BESTSELLER

BESTSELLER

THE BOOKS THAT EVERYONE READ

1900 - 1939

Claud Cockburn

SIDGWICK & JACKSON
LONDON

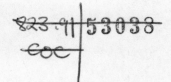
*First published in Great Britain in 1972
by Sidgwick and Jackson Limited
Copyright © Claud Cockburn 1972*

ISBN 0 283 97848 1

*Printed in Great Britain by
The Garden City Press Limited
Letchworth, Hertfordshire SG6 1JS
for Sidgwick and Jackson Limited
1 Tavistock Chambers, Bloomsbury Way
London WC1A 2SG*

CONTENTS

ILLUSTRATIONS

ACKNOWLEDGEMENTS

Acknowledgements are due to the following for granting permission to reproduce extracts from the books listed below : to the Estate of Robert Hichens for *The Garden of Allah*, published by Cedric Chivers Ltd.; to T. Fisher Unwin Ltd. (by kind permission of Ernest Benn Ltd.) for *The Blue Lagoon* by H. de Vere Stacpoole; to the Estate of Ian Hay for *The First Hundred Thousand*; to Captain Lewis C. Ricci for *The Long Trick*; to Cassell and Co. Ltd. for *Sorrell and Son* by Warwick Deeping; to Macdonald and Co. Ltd. for *The Broad Highway* by Jeffery Farnol, originally published by Sampson Low, and for *The Sheik* by E. M. Hull, originally published by Eveleigh Nash Co.; to Hodder and Stoughton Ltd. for *If Winter Comes* by A. S. M. Hutchinson; to John Murray Ltd. for *Beau Geste* by P. C. Wren; to the Estate of W. J. Locke for *The Beloved Vagabond*; to William Heinemann Ltd. for *The Constant Nymph* by Margaret Kennedy; to David Higham Associates Ltd. and Michael Arlen for *The Green Hat*; to Chatto and Windus Ltd. and Professor Ian Watt for *The Rise of the Novel*; to Jonathan Cape Ltd. and Michael S. Howard for *Jonathan Cape: Publisher*; to Weidenfeld and Nicolson Ltd. and E. J. Hobsbawn for *Industry and Empire*.

Certain sections of this book appeared in the *Observer Magazine* in November 1971.

INTRODUCTION

A good grade of opium

IN DAYS WHEN there was a period of the year called the 'silly season', and people said that nothing much ever happened in August – 1914 being an exceptional year – newspapers, British and American, filled in time and space by ringing up statesmen, trend-leaders, tycoons, gangsters, etc., to ask what was their favourite bedtime reading.

Results were predictable. Statesmen, fearing to seem aloof from the common man, said they read nothing but Westerns and detective stories. President Eisenhower was among those who said this, but in his case it was true. Tycoons and gang chiefs reported that on return from their places of business their chiefest delight was to stretch out with a really worth-while biography of a really worth-while historical figure. There was the extreme case of a banker who claimed he read nothing other than *Plato's Republic*.

Though a majority of the replies were untruthful, they were revealing. The type of lie a person tells about himself is evidently a clue to the truth. Because it was the 'silly season' no one thought of conducting this kind of enquiry seriously. It could have been more fruitful had it been directed towards finding out what all those people were reading when they were young boys and girls. What did they read during those years described loosely, because there is no way of describing them tightly, as 'formative'? To such a questionnaire there would have been a lot of fictitious replies. There might also have been a larger number of truthful ones. There are people who feel they are somehow betraying their own youth by denying the literary Gods of their childhood; it is to break a link between the men and women they are and the boys and girls they used to be.

Nobody asked him the question, but Field Marshal Lord Montgomery, in a lengthy statement given over the radio in

December 1970 and published in the *Listener*, proclaimed that a major influence, a turning-point, in his life had been his reading of Guy Thorne's novel *When It Was Dark*.

There are not many people who would be so frank as Lord Montgomery in declaring the extent to which a single and far from 'classical' novel influenced him. Everyone is safe in saying, many people quite truthfully do, that they have never been the same since reading *War and Peace*; more audacious to admit to the fact that your brainstorm on the road to Damascus was produced by *When It Was Dark*. It is an interesting and perhaps beneficial exercise for anyone to try to recall, in privacy and without risk of appearing in some poll or trend-graph, just what books really did influence him or her in childhood or early youth.

It is easier to ascertain what a mass of people were collectively reading at a given period than to get at the truth about the reading of an individual. And the reading of the mass of people is, one may suppose, more humanly, sociologically, and – in the broadest sense of the word – politically important. Even here, that is to say in terms of the 'mass reader', there is a tendency to distortion, corresponding more or less exactly to the lies told by the individual. There may even be (I say 'may' because there is no way of proving it one way or another) an element of national chauvinism in this type of distortion. Discussions of British literature in, say, the first decade of this century take more or less for granted that the English literature of the period was provided by Bennett, Shaw, Wells, Conrad, and Galsworthy, with Chesterton and Belloc on the fringes, and Kipling, essentially a nineteenth-century figure, still well up there with the leaders.

There is a sense in which the distortion is not only intelligible but partially justified. It amounts first to a literary assessment : 'These were the best British writers of the time.' Secondly, it asserts that in the long run these were the authors who counted, who moulded the national consciousness, and so on. On the other hand, it is possible that this assertion is not much justified.

The bestseller lists are an indispensable guide to problems here arising. You cannot quarrel with them. You can say that they are not an index of literary merit. You can claim that the best people did not read the bestsellers. But you cannot deny that if Book X was what a huge majority of book-buyers and book-borrowers wanted to buy or borrow in a given year, or over a period of years, then Book X satisfied a need, and expressed and realized emotions and attitudes to life which the buyers and borrowers did not find expressed or realized elsewhere. Historians and sociologists must examine innumerable sources when they are in search of the mood, the attitude, the state of mind of a nation or a class at this or that period of time. They have to look at what people really did or did not do : they went to war or they refrained from so doing; they went on strike or refused to strike; they bought significantly more or fewer bicycles than people had done a few years previously; the divorce-rate and the crime-rate rose or fell. They have also to study what people said and wrote, as distinct from what they did. There are the public speeches, the leading articles, and (when available) the personal letters and diaries. All these are indispensable. But of all indices to moods, attitudes, and, above all, aspirations, the bestseller list is one of the most reliable. There is no way of fudging it.

It is true that the England of the early twentieth century can be described, if we speak mainly of the middle class, as the England of Bennett, Shaw, and Galsworthy. But to leave it at that is a distortion. That middle-class England was also the England of Robert Hichens and *The Garden of Allah*, and of H. de Vere Stacpoole and *The Blue Lagoon*. Accurate statistics of total sales are hard to come by, and of total readership there are no statistics, but, judging by the number of editions issued and by contemporary press references, it is probable if not certain that the last two authors mentioned had a considerably larger readership than the other four put together.

I speak of the middle class because during the first decades of our century the middle class made up the bulk of the novel-buying and novel-borrowing public. It is inevitable in our society that there should be no generally agreed definition of the middle class. The only universally accepted definition is negative: the middle class is not the proletariat. At the other end of the spectrum, people have different notions as to where the middle class ends and something else – the peerage or the plutocracy for instance – begins. It may be reasonably thought that the middle-class readership I refer to ought to be subdivided into upper-middle and middle-middle class, and, furthermore, that of those subdivisions the upper-middle-class element is very much the larger. I think that is so, but can see no way of proving it one way or the other. In a matter of this kind it is rather less important that the definition be exact – which I consider to be in any case impossible – than that everyone should have a roughly accurate idea of what the definer means by it. Thus when, for convenience, I use the term 'middle class', I include in it what might also be described as the 'official class', or British Mandarinate. In pre-revolutionary China, where social distinctions were ordered more precisely than in Britain, there were nine classes of Mandarin, and, for convenience of recognition, members of each class wore a distinguishing button. Buttonless, the large mass of British officials and – more numerous still – retired officials could yet be distinguished partly by the amount of the pension drawn by each, partly by the branch of officialdom – Home Civil Service, Diplomatic Service, Consular Service, etc. – in which he functioned, or had functioned before retirement. Military officials, active or retired, also belonged to this stratum. In all cases, wives, widows, and, to a lesser extent, children of the Mandarinate must be included. Other recognizable members of the middle class as understood here include judges, barristers, solicitors, doctors, clergymen, stockbrokers, publishers, newspaper editors, and bankers between the grades of junior clerk and top-level director. The middle class contained also very many landowners and merchants, but in their case eligibility to be regarded by the student as members of the middle class depends upon how much land they owned and how much money they turned over.

It is barely necessary to point out that to speak thus of the 'middle class' does not imply that its members were uniform in their opinions or behaviour, though they were sufficiently uniform to make at least some sense of the phrase the 'middle-class vote'. Study of the bestseller throws light in particular on moods, attitudes and needs which were, at one time and another, common to large sections of the class.

To state that what masses of people read is an important index to their state of mind, to what they think and, consciously or sub-consciously, want would seem platitudinous. It is nevertheless often, in this connection, denied. The vehemence of the denials helps to prove the truth of the original platitudinous assertion.

There are people who will deny that they have done more than just glanced, or skipped through, any book which the culture-meters have not registered, or not registered high enough on the scale. This is a simple and even endearing form of intellectual snobbery. It can be seen as a kind of tribute to the classics. But these denials and repudiations can also have a somewhat deeper significance. This emerges when the reader is asked not 'Did you read and enjoy that book?' but 'Were you influenced by it?' Here the equivocations are likely to begin. We find ourselves at once in the middle of the argument which swirls around pornographic literature. Drearily familiar are the voices of those who, rather than argue that well-manufactured pornography is good (or is bad), prefer to assert that such and such a book has no influence on them, but might have a disturbing, exciting, corrupting influence on almost anyone else. Or, as is sometimes argued in the course of the wearisome type of discussion we have had over the past few years, pornography does not have any exciting, disturbing or corrupting effect upon anyone at all. So then someone legitimately asks whether this means that in the opinion of the speaker books in general, the written word, have no effect on anyone. Is the speaker saying that a person's state of mind after reading *War and Peace* or *The Diary of a Nobody* is exactly what it was before the perusal was undertaken? Is reading to be seen as a kind of chimpanzees' tea-party with people going through the motions of reading a book, turning over the pages and looking along line after line from left to right, but without internal effect? It would be easy to say that nobody in his senses would suggest such a thing. I would say it myself were I not certain that somewhere there are sincere examiners of the human make-up who believe the theory to be true.

Edmund Crispin not long ago reviewed in the *Observer* a book by Colin Watson called *Snobbery With Violence*. The book is, in my opinion, a valuable and often brilliant analysis of British thrillers and detective stories. I do not agree with all Watson's judgements, particularly his underestimation of Conan Doyle, but his book asked some interesting questions and came up with some interesting answers. Several reviewers, including Crispin, were riled. They suggested that Watson had turned light-hearted jokes into serious sociological phenomena. They had the kind of reaction some people have when anyone seeks to use the rituals of the traditional British pantomime as the basis for any kind of analysis of British sexual attitudes. True, the principal boys, etc., have been rather often examined in this sense, but this, plus the fact that the pantomime provides a lot of fun, is not a sufficient reason for asserting that the pantomime has had no serious social significance.

Crispin remarks that from Watson's book we learn that

'these rather disagreeable attitudes accurately mirror those of the middle classes to whom, predominantly, their fugitive embodiments appealed. In short, the poor old bourgeoisie has been at it again. That there is some truth in Mr Watson's thesis no one could deny. But only some. (This is a difficult assessment to clarify. How much is "some"?) And in this connection personal recollection must I think count for something. The British Middle Classes in the Twenties and Thirties, as this reviewer recalls them, were admittedly in certain ways limited and unimaginative. Overall, however, they were tolerant, kindly and humane, in actual fact almost completely devoid of the deep, dark, dank dismal complex of anti-social prejudices Mr Watson debits them with. What Mr Watson forgets is that many of their representatives were genuinely well-educated, at least up to university level : and that consequently few if any of them took seriously the sensational effusions which they borrowed from their libraries to beguile their leisure hours. They were not, that is, quite as uncritically receptive, quite as suggestible, as Mr Watson's argument requires.'

I risk, here, treating too ponderously the quick reactions of a reviewer to a book. If I use the above quotation from Crispin as a text, it is because I feel sure that his feeling about Watson's critical analysis of those thrillers and detective stories is shared by a very large number of people when they consider 'bestsellers' in general. It is a defensive reaction. The writer is concerned to defend the character and reputation of the 'British Middle Classes in the Twenties and Thirties'. I am not here concerned to attack or defend them. If the writer feels that they were 'tolerant, kindly and humane', he is certainly right to say so. There are no absolute standards of tolerance, kindliness and humaneness. If someone else chooses to say that in view of the conditions which the British middle classes condoned or fostered during that period, it would require an abnormally broad interpretation of the terms tolerant, kindly and humane to permit them to qualify for the description, then there is evidence on his side too. And by the time we are through, we shall find ourselves up to the waist in a morass of subjective judgements.

All that is irrelevant. But there is something more seriously wrong about what, just to put the thing in shorthand, we may call the 'Crispin thesis'. It suggests, though perhaps the writer did not mean to suggest quite so much, that people do not take what they read seriously; that there is no serious relationship between their own emotional or intellectual wants and the books they choose to read, the authors whose market they provide; that the bestseller is not a mirror of the mind of the reader. More than most people, the British middle classes, when conceiving themselves to have been caught out doing something not quite nice or correct, are apt to state that (a) sure enough they did it; (b) they did it either for a joke or to find out what it was that other people were so interested in; (c) the whole experience had no effect on them whatever.

And there you do get a serious distortion of history.

The bestsellers really are a mirror of 'the mind and face' of an age.

Take an example from another field of writing. At a time when the *News of the World* was demonstrably the largest-circulation newspaper in Britain, an American social prober came over to weigh up and estimate the social significance of that attested fact. He reported that although the paid *circulation* was undoubtedly around twelve million, the *readership*, so far as he could truthfully or factually state, was minuscule. Indeed, during his first week's researches he had to assume, if he believed what he was told, that it was nil. Well-to-do people bought the paper to keep the cook happy, but the cook would not dream of reading it, she just accepted it to give to her husband to keep him happy and so on and so forth. It is evident nonsense, and hoity-toity snob nonsense at that, to claim that though twelve million people bought the *News of the World*, that paper did not partially mirror the mind of the British reading public. Legitimate to claim that *The Times* was more influential in terms of diplomatic policies, the decisions of the leaders of political parties. But a great part of the infrastructure was formed by the *News of the World*. The circulation of the *News of the World* was an historical and sociological fact, and a fact more solid and undeniable than many of the speculations of the sociologists. As its editor once said, 'It is as English as roast beef'. People may be outraged at the idea. But so was Caliban when he saw his face in the mirror.

The same is to be said of the bestsellers. It is difficult to write recent British history without studying them.

To formulate the matter in this way may possibly suggest that the bestseller of a given period is to be considered solely in terms of the light it throws upon the intellectual and emotional make-up of its readers. To do so would be to create a false dichotomy between reader and writer, and also to ignore the qualities of high literary skill and craftsmanship without which a book does not reach the bestseller lists. It is true that the author of a bestseller consciously or unconsciously produces a mirror of his time. It is equally evident that only a tiny percentage of those who got their novels published in a given year had the qualities and abilities essential to the manufacture of a bestseller. It is a fact which must be recognized by those who tend to over-look or even deny the skilled craftsmanship of the bestseller be-cause, rightly or wrongly, they find it inferior in 'literary merit' to this or that other book. It is legitimate to declare that Jeffery Farnol's *The Broad Highway* is utterly inferior in literary quality to any novel of, say, Joseph Conrad. Very few people are going to quarrel with that judgement, unless out of pervers-ity or some form of inverted snobbery. It remains a fact that Farnol's work, his box of tricks if anyone prefers the phrase, is most cunningly contrived, and polished to a very high shine. The same is true in varying degrees of all those books, from *When It Was Dark* to *Rogue Herries*. It can rightly be argued that some of them, notably the military and naval stories of Ian Hay and Bartimeus, depend for their effect less upon their internal construction than upon the background against which the scene is laid. But anyone who, with the utmost goodwill towards the authors, has tried to plough through numbers of other once-popular and now forgotten novels using the First World War as background has to admit that even that back-ground is not in itself sufficiently dramatic, lurid or tragic to enable a writer without high skill to construct a readable book.

So, without having to jump very far, we come to the question of the story-teller : the bard.

Despite research, scholars have not yet decisively proved how much of Homer was written by Homer (assuming, as most ex-

perts seem now to do, that he existed) and how much was
made up by the bards as they recited and sang their tales in the
castles of the chieftains. Not open to question is the fact that
parts of the *Iliad* and the *Odyssey* are sublime, and parts, by
comparison, hack stuff, tedious, even shoddy. That is to say that
to us, reading them now, they appear tediously shoddy, and we
are right so to describe and judge them. But we would probably
be wrong to suppose that they did not go over pretty well in
those castle halls, where they appealed irresistibly to the chief
whose family was getting favourable reference, and to others
who for one reason or another wanted to hear recited and
chanted a simple, straightforward story of battle, murder or
adultery.

With the qualification that they were listened to like radio,
rather than read like books, these narrations earned just the
praises given, in their own day and in our day also, to the
bestsellers. They were 'good stories' (they were even 'rattling
good yarns'). They 'carried you along'. You 'could not put them
down' – that is to say, you did not choose to lurch out of the hall
in the middle of the twenty-fifth stanza. They were, to put it in
language so shop-soiled as to be almost dirty, 'what the public
wanted'.

With that phrase, admittedly often used to excuse the cultural
enormities of newspaper proprietors, we turn another corner
along the road trodden by the bestsellers. The author of a bestseller must be not only a man possessed of literary craftsmanship, but also a man more than usually aware of the needs of
the potential customers. It is, I suppose, just possible that a person could assess those needs and tastes without sharing them
himself, and then produce a novel fashioned to satisfy them.
Non-writing intellectuals often believe that this is frequently
done. They think the writer has 'his tongue in his cheek'.

Personally, I have sometimes wished to believe that the author
of this or that story, this or that leading article, *had* tongue in
cheek: that he was 'only doing it for the money' : that he wrote
it because his wife and children would have starved had he not.
In general, I believe the 'tongue in cheek' theory to be untrue. I
prefer the judgement of Lord Northcliffe. Some fellow fresh from
Cambridge wrote a story for the then youthful *Daily Mail* which
he felt to be jolly popular in tone : the sort of thing that would
entrance his mother's cook, and the office boys at the *Daily Mail*,

while his own friends could be assured that he had done it with his tongue in his cheek – why not take easy money off these crude Harmsworths, why shouldn't the educated upper classes despoil the Egyptians?

Northcliffe sent for him and silently shredded his written pages before his eyes.

'My boy,' he said, 'never seek to put upon the table of Demos what you would not put upon your own.'

Northcliffe, as so often in such matters, was right. Very few people, if any, can get away with what used to be called 'writing down' to the public. This has a bearing on the 'Crispin thesis'. I do not believe in the existence of superior persons who can get Demos to eat what they would reject as fare for themselves. And I do not much believe, either, in those fellows, educated up to University level, who chose books to 'beguile their leisure hours' without having any affinities with the 'dismal complex of anti-social prejudices' to be detected in the books. Inevitably, they themselves would deny all such affinities. An intellectual espied in the stalls at an Anyone-for-tennis-type drawing-room comedy will say that he wanted to see what rot people were capable of producing and furthermore had dashed into that particular theatre by accident to escape a sudden downpour of rain on Shaftesbury Avenue. If those educated men, so tolerant and humane, were repelled by, say, anti-Semitism, how come that they chose from the library shelves a book that reeked of it? There were others on the shelf. If pornography is repugnant to you, you are certainly not compelled to enter a cinema showing a pornographic film. (Unless you have to do so in the course of your duties as an investigator for some Society for the Suppression of Pornography.)

A person may truthfully claim that he is not bothered by, is – at least at the conscious level – indifferent to, this or that tendency expressed in a book, particularly in a 'mere' thriller. But the fact that, for example, anti-Semitism in the book does not bother him is already proof that he is so uncivilized as to be incapable of realizing that anti-Semitism is disgusting, dangerous, and anti-social. At the best he is so socially numbed that he does not 'see it as an issue', or else he secretly enjoys it, provided he can deny his enjoyment, putting the entire blame on the author, and claiming that he was only interested in learning who was going to shoot whom, and did the girl get raped? One needs only to imagine the reactions of a modern publisher when his author turns in a book of which the central figure and admired superman is hooked on the hard stuff. Possible, of course, but nowadays tricky. It was not so when Conan Doyle was turning Sherlock Holmes into a British national hero. This simply indicates that the original readers of the Sherlock Holmes stories were unaware of drug-addiction as a problem or issue. Sherlock's hypodermic needle, plunging in amid the very mild expostulations of Dr Watson, was made possible by the attitude of the contemporary public. The success of the stories accurately mirrors or, so to speak, reports on this element in the contemporary sociological atmosphere. And what is true of the thrillers and detective stories is equally, and probably more deeply, true of other types of fiction.

So far, to treat the sociological, historical value of the best-seller in this way is to look at a facet only of the relationship between author and reader. Setting the matter out schematically, we get: first, the existence of certain attitudes, prejudices, aspirations, etc., in the reader's conscious or subconscious mind; secondly, the existence of a *rapport*, a 'sympathy' – in the exact sense of the word – between the conscious or subconscious mind of the reader and that of the author; thirdly, the craftsmanship of the author, engaged in translating these attitudes, aspirations, etc., into acceptable fictional form; fourthly, reception by the reader of these fictional expressions.

The fifth stage in this reciprocal relationship between author and reader is a great deal more difficult to assess. In stage four the reader is represented as receiving the fictional offering or injection passively. But hardly anyone asserts that this is the end of the cycle. To do so would be to join up with those who, as noted earlier, purport to believe that a person can read a book without it having any effect whatever upon his outlook or actions. It must be conceded that this phenomenon can appear, and appear over a wide field. When phenomena like this are observed, it is commonly found that the book has not been 'read' in any meaningful sense at all. Human eyes have examined the print, human hands have turned the pages, and even half an hour after completion of the process the voice of the reader might be capable of formulating a rough synopsis of what on earth it had all been about. It is, as I have said, the parallel of that parody of human tea-drinking seen at the chimpanzees' tea-party.

The same thing may be noted in the lack of *rapport* between a given viewer and a given television programme. The programme has not penetrated meaningfully to the consciousness of the viewer. If the set had broken down during the period, showing nothing but dazzle-lines and snowflakes, it would have made no difference. This situation occurs when a particular viewer, afraid to turn the machine off for fear of missing even a second of the ensuing programme, simply sits with his eyes open in front of a screen showing a picture which he does not want to see, and certainly has not chosen to see.

'Chosen' is the operative word which links the case of the negative viewer with that of the negative reader. There can, I suppose, be no doubt that most readers and borrowers of books choose those books with more or less deliberation. The more deliberate do so, perhaps after having read a review, or heard some account or recommendation from a friend. The less deliberate are likely at least to read a page or two here and there to get the general flavour or tone before buying or borrowing. Even the least deliberate may take the precaution of seeking advice from the librarian. The negative reader is so, generally speaking, as a result of some accident. He got authors' names mixed: thought William Burroughs who wrote *The Naked Lunch* was Edgar Rice Burroughs who wrote *Tarzan of the Apes*. Whichever book he takes home, if he has the wrong one, the *rapport* is likely to be negative. Similar results may be produced by hurry at the bookstall in airport or station. In railway carriages and passenger cabins of aeroplanes, negative readers, suffering the consequences of over-hurried buying, may often be identified by the glaze of their eyes.

Still, despite their large number, instances of the reader who, usually by mishap, becomes temporarily a negative reader are relatively tiny in quantity when viewed in relation to the multi-millions of other readers who achieve some sort of relationship with the book, and upon whom the book must certainly be presumed to have some effect, however subtle.

Nobody is going to be so ham-handed as to suggest that a man or woman eagerly reading a tale of adultery, even identifying with one or other of the fictional adulterers, is going to complete the last page, let it all sink in for a minute or two, and then reach for the telephone to make illicit contact with his or her neighbour's wife or husband. It is by presenting that type of caricature of the way a book influences thought and action that some people convince themselves that the book does not influence thought and/or action at all. This latter proposition is nonsense.

Setting a good example to those who may be shy of listing the books that have influenced them, I will strain a lot of people's credulity by stating truthfully that at the age of eight I was profoundly and, I have some reason to believe, permanently influenced by the novels of Sir Walter Scott, including one or two which today I find nearly unreadable. The next influence of which I am consciously aware was that of a story called *The Pacing Mustang* by E. E. Seton-Thompson. Except that it was indeed about a pacing mustang which, fleeing from pursuers who were going to confine it in a corral and tame it, fell over a cliff in Arizona and was killed, I can recall nothing of the story. At the time that mustang incarnated for me all noble aspirations to liberty, all effort to escape restraint. The third profound influence to which I was subjected, at the age of eleven, was that of John Buchan's *The Thirty-Nine Steps*. At the time I naturally supposed that the book mirrored more or less accurately the general facts and atmosphere of adult life. Later, people were at great pains to explain to me that 'real' life was not in the least like that. It took me a long time to find out by experience and observation that 'real' life was a lot more like that than I had been told it would be.

It may be relatively – I stress 'relatively' – easy for the historian to assess the significance of a given bestseller as an expression of the prevailing political and social climate of which it is the product. To do that and no more will perhaps leave him open to the suspicion that he imagines that people think, and thus act, solely in terms of political and social relations – 'social' here being used in the sense of group, class, religious, etc., relations. What about 'strictly personal relations', 'private life', in fact? It is true, but not, in the immediate context, helpful to retort that man is a political animal, and that there is no such thing as a 'strictly personal' relationship carried on somehow independently, and hopefully oblivious, of the existing social and political setup. (It is worth noting here that, as we shall find, many of the bestsellers in the period under review express a profound wish on the part of individuals that a strictly personal relationship of the sort might be possible, somewhere, somehow. It is the yearning tragically uttered in the words of the Bing Boys, so popular with the armies: 'If you were the only girl in the world, and I was the only boy.'

But let us answer the question in the sense in which it is put. The bestsellers are, of course, rich sources of information regarding what may be called, for very rough convenience, the 'private sector' of life and love, notably love, and spilling over from there to cover the general status of women. Vividly interesting here are, for instance, the marital life of Professor Sir Robert and Lady Llwellyn in *When It Was Dark*, Sabre's domestic tensions in *If Winter Comes*, and the position of women and girls in *The Constant Nymph*. But, as is perhaps to be expected, whereas strictly political and religious notions of the period are on the whole made explicit, often principal, themes of polemic and argument, the situation on the 'private sector', including the status of women, is often taken more or less for granted, as being part of a settled order of things requiring no exposition. One may note, although this is difficult to convey without over-long quotations, the irregular recurrence of a theme in which Woman (the tone suggests the capital) is treated as being at the best an enfeebling distraction of Man from his pursuit of Truth or other worth-while endeavour, at the worst stealthily evil. The ethic of Calvin, Knox, and such, not to mention Anglo-Roman versions of attitudes supposedly prevalent in the Roman Republic and Empire, were both powerful in British culture of the period. It is a point at which that much-flagellated whipping-boy, the British Public School, must come up for a deserved beating. It may be remarked that in the early twentieth century, the corrosive influence of women consisted chiefly in their inability to understand a man's deeper feelings. Mabel Sabre in *If Winter Comes* is an outstanding example. Her lecherous feelings for a retired military man, whom she marries as soon as she is rid of Sabre, are muted throughout the book, and are not a factor in Sabre's attitude to her.

Obviously the best-selling historical romances did not shed so much direct light on personal behaviour at the time they were written. Obliquely they shed a lot. True, the historical romancer does not purport to be dealing with the manners and customs of his contemporaries. He is reporting events in an imaginary world.

But he and his contemporary readers have constructed that
world and peopled it with figures of their own devising. The way
they ensure or demand that these puppets should behave is
inevitably an indication of their attitudes to human behaviour
in the 'private sector' in their own day.

So far as the material apparatus of life is concerned, a curious
fact emerges. One might expect that in a novel written, say, in
1910 the difference between then and now in the material
apparatus of living would be as obtrusive as the funny hats and
trousers to be seen in primitive newsreels. No mass-produced
motor-cars, few telephones, no air transport at all. The fact I
describe as curious is that this sort of enormous difference between our material situation and that of the people of 1910
seems so very faintly noticeable. The moments are strangely
rare at which one feels that if one or other of the characters had
been on the telephone or able to get from London to Paris in
three-quarters of an hour, his or her behaviour, and the movement of the plot, would have been much affected. (This does
not apply to the historical romances. Intercepted missives are
there very useful properties, for letters were more often intercepted than telephones are tapped, even now.) A notable
exception to the point about the telephone is to be remarked in
If Winter Comes. Had Lady Tybar had the telephone at
Northropps, her country mansion, she would not have had to
write the brief note to Sabre which triggered off so much trouble.

Paradoxically, but intelligibly, the sense of strangeness, of
something odd or lacking in the technological set-up, seems to
increase slightly rather than decrease the nearer we get to our
own period. This sensation of increasing strangeness is commonly
experienced by people looking at old newsreels or photograph
albums. The hats of ten years ago look queerer than those of
fifty or sixty years ago. Presumably in the case of pictures, as of
books, this occurs because in the nearer pictures or descriptions
there is enough to lead us to assume that these people are
inhabiting a world almost identical with our own; evidence that
they are not, however trivial, produces a jolt. Where earlier
periods are concerned there is less expectation of similarity.

The books dealing directly with the First World War, for
instance Hay's *The First Hundred Thousand*, are inevitably
exceptional in this respect. One can hardly be unaware of the
difference between what explosives and airborne machinery can

do now and what they could do then. The same would be true
if the books in question had dealt with, say, a mining village or
dockyard.

The reader of this book will quickly note that two, three or
even more of his favourite bestsellers of the past have been
mistakenly, arbitrarily and unaccountably omitted. He will feel
that those books – possibly 'formative' in his life – are more
basically significant and revealing than those discussed here. If
we substitute 'equally' for 'more', I would probably agree.
Indeed, I have done so, by word and letter, to many acquain-
tances who, partly to help me and partly to try to get justice
done to their favourites, have sent me truly significant books,
and even taken time off to read long passages of an illuminating
kind aloud to me. I hope that this book will renew and possibly
deepen their interest in their own selection.

My own choice is, of course, arbitrary. It is not, however, by
any means haphazard. An essential criterion is that the books
should be of a kind which a high proportion of the relevant
public would either buy or write down on library lists. A rough
guide to such books is provided by contemporary book reviews.
Very few books that were seriously reviewed could become
bestsellers. But a book which was seriously, even though sometimes fatuously, reviewed and became a bestseller was one that
the public was taking seriously : talking about, thinking about,
inwardly more or less digesting. It was an event, with consequences.

This criterion decided me to exclude, after hesitation, the
Tarzan books.

Detective stories and thrillers, shockers, suspense novels depend
for their appeal on so many elements peculiar to the *genre* that
to include them, despite their significance, would have produced
the equivalent of an urban sprawl, exhibiting an unmanageable
variety of styles and functions. For two admirable studies of
the *genre* I recommend Richard Usborne's *Clubland Heroes*
(Constable, 1953) and Colin Watson's *Snobbery With Violence*
(Eyre and Spottiswoode, 1971).

Everyone can recite a long list of American books, with
American settings, which often outsold British contemporaries,
particularly in the nineteen-twenties and -thirties. To have
included them would have widely and fruitfully extended our
knowledge of the wants of the British middle class. It would

have extended it over an additional hundred and fifty pages and monstrously increased the cost of this book.

The book ends where it does for two reasons. The first is as obvious as the reply of the able-bodied man in the pre-conscription days of 1914 to the question why he did not join the Army. 'Well, you see,' he said, 'there's this war.' The second reason is less easily defined; and it is best defined in a negative way. During the last three decades, give or take a quinquennium or so, the film industry and television have more and more often been called in not only to attend at the birth of a bestseller, but to keep a close eye on its pre-natal care, and even to arrange its conception. And the arrangements for mass printing of the paperback edition can be made, in consultation with the film-makers, in the knowledge that the book will be filmed. In the earlier period, during which all the books mentioned here were published, the films were made only after the book had already forced its way, with the aid of publishers' skill, publishers' resources, and the huge, always present, element of luck, on to the bestseller lists.

The term 'bestseller' is often used in a pejorative sense. It evokes the notion that more people read bad books than good books, and the suggestion, both snobbish and misleading, that almost any well-selling book must be of inferior quality (unless the author is at least as dead as Dickens or Tolstoy). It is also true that in our cultural climate green bay trees often flourish exceedingly while nobler plants wither as soon as planted.

Contemplating the bestsellers one may recall the phrase of Marx, so well-worn and so misused. His remark that 'religion is the opium of the people' is customarily quoted out of context as a coarsely simple anti-religious jibe. He was writing of the misery of the workers' life in the factory towns of the Industrial Revolution. In China, the coolie found solace in opium. In England, Marx wrote, religion is 'The heart of a heartless world, the soul of soulless conditions; it is the opium of the people.'

It may well be that in a better world many of the bestsellers would have been seen as superfluous or even contemptible. But, things being what they were, they did, at worst, produce a good grade of opium.

The horror of it all

'THE MOST DARING and original novel of the century is *When It Was Dark* by Guy Thorne.' Since the date of publication was 1903, this claim by the publishers might look as cautious as a bet on a cert. How many still more daring and original novels had had an opportunity to be issued since the twentieth century began?

The answer is that although the publishers' statement might in one sense appear somewhat absurd, it was not merely true, but stayed true, or as true as any such assertion can be held to be, for years and years. *When It Was Dark* was one of the most significant works of the Edwardian and early Georgian eras. It was read by people who found little to excite them in the novels of the period which have, as the saying goes, 'lived'. It is, by any standards, a *tour de force* of extraordinary vivacity and skill. And its stew of spicy cunning, gross pomposity, wild melodrama, heavy religiosity, anti-Semitism and acute class-consciousness, has a niff and flavour which re-create that not very distant age more vividly and authentically than many far better books.

An early and useful summary of this plot was given by the Bishop of London, who, soon after the book was published, preached about it at Westminster Abbey. He said :

'I wonder whether any of you have read that remarkable work of fiction entitled *When It Was Dark*? It paints, in wonderful colours, what it seems to me the world would be if for six months, as in the story is supposed to be the case, owing to a gigantic fraud, the Resurrection might be supposed never to have occurred, and as you feel the darkness creeping round the world, you see how Woman in a moment loses the best friend she ever had, and crime and violence increase in every part of the world. When you see how darkness settles down

upon the human spirit, regarding the Christian record as a
fable, then you quit with something like adequate thanks-
giving, and thank God it is light because of the awful darkness when it was dark.'

Guy Thorne, a prolific novelist and journalist whose name
was Ranger-Gull, opens his book, subtitled *The Story of a Great
Conspiracy*, in the study of Mr Byars, Vicar of St Thomas's,
Walktown. (The church itself has long rows of cushioned seats
each labelled with the name of the person who rented it. The
congregation consists of 'the moderately prosperous and wholly
vulgar Lancashire people'.

To the distress of Mr Byars,

'Walktown was a stronghold of the Unitarians. The wealthy
Jews of two generations back, men who made vast fortunes
in the Black Valley of the Irwell, had chosen Walktown to
dwell in. Their grandsons had found it more politic to abjure
their ancient faith. A few had become Christians – at least
in name, inasmuch as they rented pews at St Thomas's – but
others had compromised by embracing a faith, or rather a
dogma, which is simply Judaism without its ritual and cere-
monial obligations. The Baumanns, the Hildersheimers, the
Steinhardts, flourished in Walktown... The vicar had two
strong elements to contend with... on the one hand the
Lancashire natives, on the other the wealthy Jewish families.
The first were hard, uncultured people, hating everything
that had not its origin and end in commerce. They disliked
Mr Byars because he was a gentleman and because he was
educated.'

This Ambrose Byars is in bad trouble because his curate, Basil
Gortre, who is engaged to his daughter Helena, is leaving for a
London parish and it is going to be hard to replace him : 'The
best men would not come to the North. Men of family, with
decent degrees, Oxford men, Cambridge men, accustomed to
decent society and intellectual friends, knew far too much to
accept a title in the Manchester district.'

No wonder the vicar is worried. But Helena knows of a
remedy. Entering the study she announces: 'I've brought *Punch*,
father, it's just come. Leave your work now and enjoy yourself

for half an hour before dinner. Basil will be here by the time you're finished.'

Anyone today can get an easy laugh out of the thought of a serious man's serious troubles being in any way alleviated by a half-hour with the latest issue of *Punch*. But there is more to it than a laugh. The point is that Thorne had his facts right. A re-reading of *Punch* for the years, say, 1900 to 1903 proves it. *Punch*, the fun-bible of the genteel (as distinct from 'wholly vulgar') section of the British middle class, portrayed as exactly as does Thorne the atmosphere of a period which, we have to keep reminding ourselves, was part of our own century. A period, that is to say, when 'men accustomed to decent society' would only under great pressure venture much north of the Thames Valley, and people with names such as Baumann or Hildersheimer were automatically suspect of undermining the national culture. ('It was', says Thorne in one of his frequent anti-cultural asides, 'people of this class who supported the magnificent concerts in the Free Trade Hall at Manchester, who bought the pictures and read the books. They had brought an alien culture to the neighbourhood.')

Basil Gortre, curate, now arrives. He is going to be the hero of the book, so he 'had private means of his own, and belonged to an old west country family'. 'The three sat down to dine. It was a simple meal, some fish, cold beef and a pudding, with a bottle of beer for the curate and a glass of claret for the vicar. The housemaid did not wait upon them, for they found the meal more intimate and enjoyable without her.' The fact of not having a servant to wait upon three people is thus seen as a very slight, though intelligible, eccentricity. The 'simplicity' of the meal itself, just three courses with beer and wine, has to be seen in contrast to the abominable sensuality of the food savoured by one or two of the villains soon to be encountered.

It is learned that Gortre is to share rooms in the Inns of Court with Harold Spence, who is 'writing leaders for the *Daily Wire* and doing very well', and a famous archaeologist named Cyril Hands who, the vicar recalls, recently discovered some inscriptions in 'the place which is thought may be Golgotha, you know'.

Harmless enough, you might think nowadays, to announce to your fiancée and your future father-in-law that you proposed to live in Lincoln's Inn with a distinguished archaeologist and the leader-writer of *The Times* – for as later events indicate the

Daily Wire is a thinnish disguise for *The Times*. But not so in
1903.

' "Isn't it just a little, well, bachelor?" said Helena, rather
nervously.

Gortre smiled at the question.

"No, dear," he said, "I don't think you need be afraid . . .
You don't know Harold. He is quite *bourgeois* in his habits;
despite his intellect hates a muddle; always dresses extremely
well, and goes to church like any married man." [The idea
that any ordinary man of 'intellect' might be expected to love
a muddle is characteristic.]

"The days when you couldn't be a genius without being
dirty", said the Vicar, "are gone. I am glad of it. I was staying at St Ives last summer, where there is quite an artistic
settlement. All the painters carried golf clubs and looked like
professional athletes. They drink Bohea in Bohemia now." '

Helena is reassured. She leaves the vicar and curate to smoke
their pipes and talk, principally, of anti-Christ. Gortre is full of
foreboding.

'Gortre stood by the mantelshelf, leaning his elbow upon it.
One of the ornaments of the mantel was a head of Christ,
photographed on china, from Murillo, and held in a large
silver frame like a photograph frame.

There came a sudden knock at the door. It startled Gortre
and he moved suddenly. His elbow slid along the marble of
the shelf and dislodged the picture which fell upon the floor
and was broken into a hundred pieces, crashing loudly upon
the fender.

The housemaid who had knocked stood for a moment
looking with dismay upon the breakage. Then she turned to
the vicar.

"Mr Schuabe from Mount Prospect to see you, Sir," she
said; "I've shown him into the drawing-room." '

This Constantine Schuabe is a multi-millionaire, an M.P. of
overpowering intellect and eloquence; he owns the *Daily Wire*
and is 'one of the ten most striking-looking men in England'.
Standing motionless now in the vicar's drawing-room,

. .

I
Guy Thorne
From *The Complete Wildfowler*

2
Robert Hichens
Radio Times Hulton Picture Library

3
H. de Vere Stacpoole
Hughes Massie Limited

'The man was tall . . . and the heavy coat of fur he was
wearing increased the impression of proportioned size, of mas-
siveness, which was part of his personality. His hair was a
very dark red, smooth and abundant . . . His features were
Semitic, but without a trace of that fulness, and sometimes
coarseness, which often marks the Jew who has come to the
middle period of life. The eyes were large and black, but
without animation in ordinary use-and-wont. They did not
light up as he spoke, but yet the expression was not veiled or
obscured. They were coldly, terribly *aware*, with something of
the sinister and untroubled regard one sees in a reptile's eyes.
   Most people, with the casual view, called him merely
indomitable, but there were others who thought they read
deeper and saw something evil and monstrous about the
man . . . now and again, two or three people would speak of
him to each other without reserve, and on such occasions they
generally agreed to this feeling of the sinister and malign.'

What, in fact, we have here is the first appearance in full rig
of a figure who is to reappear with fascinating frequency in
British literature right through the first third of the century, most
notably in the novels of John Buchan. The social significance of
his popularity with the British middle class is profound, particularly when it is noted that, at a slightly later stage, and not by
any means in fiction alone, he is discovered among the principal
Devil-figures of Nazi mythology.
   At first sight it would seem difficult to give any sort of credibility to a figure who is at the same time a multi-millionaire and
a devilish and deliberate agent for the destruction of established
society. (He is sometimes a multi-millionaire and a Bolshevik,
sometimes a multi-millionaire and an anarchist. The label is not
of great importance, provided it describes something terribly
subversive.) He is, in fact, a figure straight out of the Protocol
of the Elders of Zion.
   But for scores of thousands, perhaps hundreds of thousands,
of people, he was not merely credible; his existence was a social
and emotional necessity.
   As a class, the middle class was menaced on two fronts. The
threat from below by the working class was increasing in fact
and, so to speak, in visibility. It could be discerned as an
insistent, persisting threat by people who twenty years earlier

2—B * *

might have seen it as a passing wave of agitation. The British industrial crisis, which in less than ten years was going to reach dimensions seeming to justify those who thought the danger of civil war more immediate than that of international war, was already developing – clearly in the sight of some, to others as a bugbear, real part of the time, and part of the time susceptible of being dismissed as an ugly hallucination.

On the other front were the forces known collectively to the middle class as the 'New Rich'. In one sense, they were not so new as all that. They had been detected, for instance, those threatening, subversive hordes of Midian, prowling around the English Way of Life in Trollope's great sociological novel *The Way We Live Now*, published in the 1870s. The figure of Melmotte, so unimaginably rich, so devilish crooked, already lowered and lurched among established institutions. He was a power in the Tory Party. Royalty went to his house.

The phenomenon, however, though ideologically frightful, was not immediately and materially relevant to the lives of most people of the middle class. They felt that they, like the Empire, were at least stable, and perhaps on the up-grade. By the turn of the century this confidence had been badly shaken. It may be supposed that only pundits (and by no means all of them) perceived that the Empire had already passed its zenith, and that the forces which had brought it into being were shifting direction; the character of the central British economy was so changing that the entire structure, still outwardly as stable as ever, was in fact precarious. But the most recondite observations of the pundits are rarely hidden so deep as is imagined. Like other great State secrets, they leak, they make a smell in the air. The man in the street or the lending library may not know what makes the smell, but he knows there is a bit of a stink somewhere. Hobsbawm, in *Industry and Empire*, remarks that

'The somnolence of the economy was already obvious in British society in the last decades before 1914. Already the rare dynamic entrepreneurs of Edwardian Britain were, more often than not, foreigners or minority groups (the increasingly important German-Jewish financiers who provided the excuse for much of the pervasive anti-Semitism of the period, the Americans so important in the electrical industry, the Germans in chemicals.)'

Like Melmotte earlier, the New Rich of early twentieth century were sometimes mysteriously, sometimes obtrusively, powerful in politics, Like him, they were cultivated by Royalty. To put it plainly, they mucked about with the value of money, notably by their demonic abracadabra on the Stock Exchange. Even if a majority of them and their hangers-on were English by birth, their interests were not identical with the interests of the English middle class.

A very large segment of the middle class lived, wholly or in part, on fixed incomes. And the activities both of the New Rich and of the proletariat were seen as jointly responsible for that most immediate and damaging of developments, the rise in the cost of living.

In facing the threat from the proletariat, the middle class found itself in an ideological dilemma. It was a necessary part of its creed that the British working man was good – often a genuine Tory – at heart. Why then did he make unreasonable demands, why did he threaten to strike or actually strike, when strikes could surely be seen as disastrous to 'the interests of the community as a whole'?

It was convenient, and in a sense comforting, to reply that he did so because he was the dupe and victim of foreign agitators, with foreign ideas. And whence did these agitators, who must evidently be operating on a gigantic scale, get their money? Where could they be getting it from except the devious, over-brained, ruthless and essentially un-English Jewish financiers? Thus a composite figure was found who combined the worst features of both the threatening elements.

The German, and indeed most of the Western, intelligentsia were incredulous when Hitler set out to prove that Wall Street and the Communists, all run by Jews, were in essence the same people pursuing identical objectives. For a dangerously long time the intelligentsia simply refused to believe that so preposterous a notion could deceive anyone but the infantile or the senile. Much too late, this same intelligentsia were forced to realize that millions of people could be brought to believe not only that, but also to believe, as the Nazi Press told them to during the Second World War, that President Roosevelt was a Jew whose real name was Rosenfeld, and was acting in collaboration with Communists (whose leader's first name was Joseph) to bring about the destruction of Western society.

With this fairly recent phenomenon in mind, we can better understand the credibility of Constantine Schuabe, and the impact of *When It Was Dark.*

Enter (in London) villain Number Two, or the Second Murderer. This is Robert Llwellyn, internationally famous *savant* in charge of the Palestinian section of the British Museum. He is described as being 'that almost inhuman phenomenon, a sensualist with a soul'. In his room at the Museum he has just received the news that he is about to be knighted for services rendered to science, archaeology, scriptural knowledge and so on. But he too has troubles of a kind with which it might be difficult for, say, an Oxford don of the 1970s to identify. He is leading a double life.

> 'The lofty scientific world of which he was an ornament, had no points of contact with that other and unspeakable half life. Rumours had been bruited, things said in secret by envious and less distinguished men, but they had never harmed him ... What did it matter if smaller people with forked tongues hissed horrors of his private life? The other circles – the lost slaves of pleasure – knew him well and were content.'

What then were the horrors so hissed? They consisted in the fact that, although a married man, he kept a mistress. And this mistress was a music-hall actress so well known that her picture appeared on cigarette cards. He kept her in Bloomsbury Court Mansions. One does not today associate Bloomsbury with luxurious vice, but that, in 1903, was what it meant. The room of

> 'one of London's popular favourites, Miss Gertrude Hunt, reeked with a well-known perfume, an evil, sickly smell of ripe lilies and the acrid smoke of Egyptian tobacco ... The room would have struck an ordinary visitor with a sense of nausea almost like a physical blow. There was something sordidly shameless about it. The vulgarest and most material of Circes held sway among all this gaudy and lavish disorder. The most sober-minded and innocent-minded man, brought suddenly into such a place, would have known it instantly for what it was and turned to fly as from a pestilence.'

It should be said here that despite a Jewish look, a vulgarly cockney accent (in which she sings with enormous success a song called 'The Coon of Coons') and her sexual immorality, she turns up trumps in the end, pushed along by Basil Gortre and the knowledge that she is soon going to die of an incurable 'internal disease'.

Just before venturing into this den in Bloomsbury, we are offered a *vignette* of Prof. Llwellyn's home life. Here again, the point is that Guy Thorne's public of 1903 obviously found the picture quite credible. So much so, in fact, that the author does not find it necessary to suggest that there was anything more than a little unusual about it. In the 1970s the thing would take a good deal of explaining, and the characters concerned would have to be represented as fugitives from a sanatorium. How otherwise account for the fact that Mrs Llwellyn does not divorce the Professor?

'They had been married for fifteen years. For fourteen of them he had hardly ever spoken to her except in anger at some household accident. On her own private income of six hundred a year she had to do what she could to keep the house going. Llwellyn never gave her anything of the thousand a year which was his salary at the Museum, and the greater sums he earned by his salary outside it. She knew no one. The Professor went into none but official society, and indeed but few of his colleagues knew that he was a married man. He treated the house as an hotel, sleeping there occasionally, breakfasting and dressing. His private rooms were the only habitable part of the house. All the rest was old, faded and without comfort. Mrs Llwellyn spent most of her life with the two servants in the kitchen. She always swept and tidied her husband's rooms herself. That afternoon she had built and coaxed the fire with her own hands. She slept in a small room at the top of the house, next to the maids, for company. This was her life.'

Our sensualist with a soul, on arrival at Bloomsbury Court Mansions, is so troubled that, despite having eaten nothing but a snack of soup, fish and cheese, he is unable to eat the supper prepared for him by the vulgar and material Circe. The reason for this trouble is that he is being sexually blackmailed by Miss Hunt and financially blackmailed by the man Schuabe, now resident at the Hotel Cecil, next door to the Savoy, overlooking the Thames, and arranging for getting rid of Christianity and all that that implies.

Schuabe has written to the Professor demanding that he pay back loans from Schuabe of which 'the principal and interest now total the sum of fourteen thousand pounds'.

The man Schuabe writes :

'It would be superfluous to point out to you what bankruptcy would mean to you in your position. Ruin would be the only word. And it would be no ordinary bankruptcy. I have by no means an uncertain idea where these large sums have gone, and my knowledge can hardly fail to be shared by others in London Society. [I.e. He will tell London Society about Gertrude Hunt.]

I have still a chance to offer you, however, and perhaps you will find me by no means the tyrant you think. There are certain services which you can do me, and which, if you fall in with my views, will not only wipe off the few thousands of your indebtedness, but will provide you with a capital sum which will place you above the necessity for any such financial manœuvres in the future as your – shall I say *infatuation* – has led you to resort to in the past. If you care to lunch with me in my rooms at the Hotel Cecil at two o'clock the day after tomorrow – Friday – we may discuss your affairs quietly. If not then I must refer you to my solicitors entirely. Yours sincerely, Constantine Schuabe.'

So what is our man Schuabe going to get for his many thousand pieces of gold? Simply this : On grounds of alleged ill-health the Professor is to get one year's leave of absence from the British Museum.

He will proceed to Jerusalem.

With his unparalleled skill and the help of an enormous bribe from Schuabe to a corruptible Greek called Ionides, a man much esteemed by the Palestine Exploration Society, he will then forge, in a tomb just outside Jerusalem, a certain inscription.

The nature of this inscription? It is nothing less than a message from Joseph of Arimathea, admitting that he, Joseph, stole the body of Christ and hid it in this same tomb. So that when the disciples thought that Christ had risen from the dead, they were victims of a well-meant deception by Joseph of Arimathea. There had been no Resurrection. The body had merely been secretly transferred from one tomb to another. The entire Christian world had been the victim of this hoax.

They did not have radium tests in those days, capable of deciphering the antiquity or otherwise of such an inscription or of 'the slight mould on the stone slab which may or may not be' (as the *Daily Wire* was to announce later) 'that of a decomposed body'. All the same, it certainly took fifty thousand pounds worth of the Professor's skill to fake the thing so that it was going, a bit later, to fool all the greatest Palestinian experts in the world, including archaeologist Hands.

For, obviously enough, it was not going to be Llwellyn who would make the historic discovery. The thing that was going to change the history of the world would come to light as a result of the honest exploratory labours of honest men like Hands.

And so, in the fullness of time and exactly in accordance with the malign calculation of Devil-man Schuabe, it came to pass. It is naturally difficult in a summary to do any kind of justice to Guy Thorne's capacity for the creation of suspense. To convey it one must quote at some length the chapter in which the news of the supposed discovery in Jerusalem reaches London. Harold Spence, you will remember, is a leader-writer for the *Daily Wire*. One of his room-mates, Cyril Hands, is agent of the Palestine Exploration Society. Hands has recently left for Palestine on the business of the Society. The reader is of course already aware of the nature and the successful carrying out of the tremendous plot concocted by Schuabe and Sir Robert Llwellyn, but nobody else in the civilized world is aware of the fearful time-bomb ticking away beneath them. With admirable skill Thorne delays the final revelation with what might otherwise be a pedestrian account of a day in the life of Harold Spence.

'One Wednesday – he remembered the day afterwards – Spence woke about midday. He had been late at the office the night before and afterwards had gone to a club, not going to bed till after four.

He heard the "laundress" [charwoman] moving about the chambers preparing his breakfast. He shouted to her and in a minute or two she came in with his letters and a cup of tea.

She went to the window and pulled up the blind, letting a dreary grey-yellow December light into the room. "Nasty day, Mrs Buscall?" he said, sipping his tea. "It is so, sir," the woman said, a lean kindly-faced London drudge, caught in Drury Lane. "Gives me a frog in my throat all the time, this fog does . . . letter from Mr Cyril, I see, sir," she remarked. Mrs Buscall loved the archaeologist with more strenuousness than her other two charges: the unusual and mysterious has a real fascination for a certain type of un-educated Cockney brain. Hands's rare sojourns at the chambers, the Eastern dresses and pictures in his room, his strange and perilous life, as she considered it, in the veritable Bible land where Satan actually roamed the desert in the form of a lion seeking whom he might devour, all these stimulated her crude imagination and brought colour into the dreary purlieus of Drury Lane. Most of the women around Mrs Buscall drank gin. The doings of Cyril Hands were sufficient tonic for her.

Spence glanced at the bulky package with the Turkish stamps and peculiar aroma, which the London fog had not yet killed, of ships and alien sounds. Hands was a good correspondent. Sometimes he sent general articles on the work he was doing, not too technical, and Ommaney, the editor of Spence's paper, used and paid well for them.

But on this morning Spence did not feel inclined to open the packet. It could wait. He was not in the humour for it now. It would be too tantalizing to read of those deep skies like a hard hollow turquoise, of the flaming white sun, the white mosque and minarets throwing purple shadows round the cypresses and olives . . . After breakfast, the lunchtime of most of the world, he found it impossible to settle down to anything. He was not due at the office that night and the long hours without the excitement of his work stretched rather hopelessly before him. He thought of paying calls in the various parts of the West End where he had friends whom he had rather neglected of late. But he dismissed that idea when it came, for he did not feel as if he could make himself very agreeable to anyone. He half thought of running down to Brighton, fighting the cold bracing sea winds on the lawns at Hove and returning the next day. He was certainly out of sorts – liverish, no doubt – and the solution to his difficulties presented itself to him in the project of a Turkish bath. He put his correspondence into the pocket of his overcoat to be read at leisure and drove to a Hammam in Jermyn Street. The physical warmth, the silence, the dim lights and oriental decorations induced a supreme sense of comfort and *bien être*. It brought Constantinople back to him in vague reverie.

Perhaps, he thought, the Turkish bath in London is the only easy way to obtain a sudden and absolute change of environment. Nothing else brings detachment so readily, so instinct with change and the unusual. In the delightful languor he passed from one dim chamber to another, lying prone in the great heat which surrounded him like a cloak. Then the vigorous kneading and massage, the gradual toning and renovating of each joint and muscle till he stood drenched in aromatic foam, a new fresh physical personality ... at four a slippered attendant brought him a sole and a bottle of yellow wine and after the light meal he fell once more into a placid restorative sleep.

And all the while the letter from Jerusalem was in his overcoat pocket, forgotten, hung in the entrance hall. The thing which was to alter the lives of thousands and tens of thousands, that was to bring a cloud over England more dark and menacing than it had ever known, lay there with its stupendous message, its relentless influence, while outside the church bells all over London were tolling for Evensong. At length, as night was falling, Spence went out into the lighted streets with their sudden roar of welcome. He was immensely refreshed, his thoughts moved quickly and well, depression had left him and the activity of his brain was unceasing.

He turned into St James's Street where his club was, intending to find somebody who would come to a music-hall with him. There was no one he knew intimately in the smoking room but soon after he arrived Lambert, one of the deputy curators from the British Museum, came in. Spence and Lambert had been at Marlborough together. Spence asked Lambert, who was in evening dress, to be his companion. "Sorry, I can't, old man," he answered, "I've got to dine with my uncle, Sir Michael. It's a bore of course but it's policy. The place will be full of High Church bishops and minor Cabinet ministers and people of that sort. I only hope old Ripon will be there, he's my uncle's tame vicar you know, uncle runs an expensive church like some men run a theatre, for he's always bright and amusing . . . sorry I can't come, awful bore. I've had a tiring day too and a ballet would be refreshing. The governor's been in a state of filthy irritation and nerves for the last fortnight."

"Sir Robert Llwellyn, isn't it?"

"Yes, he's my chief and a very good fellow too as a rule. He went away for several months, you know, travelled abroad for his health. [The reader of course is aware of the real purpose of Sir Robert's excursion.] When he first came back three months ago he looked as fit as a fiddle and seemed awfully pleased with himself all round. But lately he's been decidedly off colour. He seems worried about something, does hardly any work and he always seems waiting and looking out for a coming event. He bothers me out of my life, always coming into my room and talking about nothing, or speculating upon the possibility of all sorts of new discoveries which will upset everyone's theories."

"I met him in Dieppe in the Spring. He seemed all right then, just at the beginning of his leave."

"Well, he's certainly not that now, worse luck, and confound him. He interferes with my work no end."

It was after seven o'clock. Spence wasn't hungry yet, the light meal in the Hammam had satisfied him. He resolved to go to the Empire alone, not because the idea of going seemed very attractive but because he had planned it and could substitute no other way of spending the evening for the first determination. So about nine o'clock he strolled into the huge garish music hall. He went into the Empire and already his contentment was beginning to die away again. The day seemed a day of trivialities, a sordid uneventful day of London gloom which he had vainly tried to disperse with little futile rockets of amusement. He sat down in a stall and watched a clever juggler doing wonderful things with billiard balls. After the juggler a coarsely handsome Spanish girl came upon the stage – he remembered her at La Scala in Paris. She was said to be one of the beauties of Europe and a King's favourite.

After the Spanish woman there were two men, "Brothers"

someone. One was disguised as a donkey, the other as a tramp and together they did laughable things.

With a sigh he went upstairs and moved slowly through the thronged promenade. The hard faces of the men and women repelled him. One elderly Jewish-looking person reminded him of a great grey slug. He turned into the American Bar at one extremity of the horseshoe. It was early yet and the big room pleasantly cool was quite empty. A man brought him a long particoloured drink.

He felt the pressure of the packet in his pocket. It was Cyril Hands's letter he found as he took it out. He thought of young Lambert at the club, a friend of Hands and fellow worker in the same field, and languidly opened the letter.

Two women came in and sat at a table not far from him as he began to read. He was the only man in the place and they regarded him with a tense conscious interest. They saw him open a bulky envelope with a careless manner. He would look up soon, they expected.

But as they watched they saw a sudden swift contraction of the brows, a momentous convulsion of every feature. His head bent lower towards the manuscript. They saw that he became very pale.

In a minute or two what had at first seemed a singular paleness became a frightful ashen colour. "That Johnny's going to be ill," one of the women said to another. As she spoke they saw the face change. A lurid excitement burst out upon it like a flame. The eyes glowed, the mouth settled into swift purpose.

Spence took up his hat and left the room with quick decided steps. He threaded his way through the crowd round the circle, like a bed of orchids surrounded by heavy poisonous scents, and almost ran into the street. A cab was waiting. He got into it and inspired by his words and appearance the man drove furiously down dark Garrick Street and the blazing Strand towards the offices of the *Daily Wire*. The great building of dressed stone which stood in the middle of Fleet Street was dark. The advertisement hall and business offices were closed. The journalist turned down a long corridor with doors on either side . . . at the extreme end he opened a door and passing round a red baize screen flung himself in on Ommaney's room, the centre of the great web of brains and machinery which daily gave the *Wire* to the world. Ommaney's room was very large, warm and bright – it was also extremely tidy. The writing table had little on it save the great blotting pad and an inkstand, the books on chairs and shelves were neatly arranged . . . Ommaney was slim and pale, carefully dressed and of medium height. He did not look very old. His moustache was golden and carefully tended, his pale honey-coloured hair waved over a high white forehead.

"I shall want an hour," Spence said. "I've just got what may be the most stupendous news any newspaper has ever published."

The editor looked up quickly. A flash of interest passed over his pale immobile face and was gone. He knew that if Spence spoke like this the occasion was momentous. He looked at his watch. "Is it news for tonight's paper?" he said. "No," answered Spence, "I'm the only man in England I think who has it yet. We shall gain nothing by printing tonight but we must settle our course of action at once. That won't wait. You'll understand when I explain . . ." Spence took a chair opposite. He seemed dazed. He was trembling with excitement. His face was pale with it, yet above and beyond this agitation there was almost fear in his eyes.

"It's a discovery in Palestine – at Jerusalem," he said in a low vibrating voice, spreading out the thin crackling sheets of foreign notepaper on his knee and arranging them in order. "You know Cyril Hands, the agent of the Palestine Exploring Fund?" "Yes, quite well by reputation," said Ommaney, "and I've met him once or twice. Very sound man." "These papers are from him. They seem to be of tremendous importance, of a significance that I can hardly grasp yet." "What is the nature of them?" asked the editor, rising from his chair, powerfully affected in his turn by Spence's manner. Harold put his hand up to his throat, pulling at his collar, the apple moved up and down convulsively.

"The tomb!" Spence gasped. "The Holy Tomb!"

"What do you mean?" asked Ommaney. "Another supposed burial place of Christ – like *The Times* business when they found the Gordon tomb, and Canon MacColl wrote such a lot?"

His face fell a little. This, though interesting enough and fine news copy, was less than he hoped.

"No, no," cried Spence, getting his voice back at last and speaking like a man in acute physical pain. *"A new tomb has been found, there is an inscription in Greek, written by Joseph of Arimathea, and there are other traces."*

His voice failed him. *"Go on, man, go on,"* said the editor.

"The inscription – tells that – Joseph took the body of Jesus – from his own garden tomb – he hid it in this place – the disciples never knew – it is a confession."

Ommaney was as white as Spence now.

"There are other contributory proofs," Spence continued. *"Hands says that it is certain. All the details are here, read –"*

Ommaney stared fixedly at his lieutenant.

"Then if this is true," he whispered, *"it means?"*

"THAT CHRIST NEVER ROSE FROM THE DEAD. THAT CHRISTIANITY IS ALL A LIE."

Spence slipped back in his chair a little and fainted.'

After Spence has been partially revived with brandy the editor soliloquizes aloud on the situation.

' "Of course I and you are hardly competent to judge of the value of this communication. To me, speaking as a layman, it seems extremely clear. But we must of course see a specialist before publishing anything. If this news is true, and I will give all I am worth if it were not, though I am no Christian, of course you realise that the future history of the world is changed. I hold in my hand something that will come to millions and millions of people as an utter extinction of hope and light. It's impossible to say what will happen. Moral law will be abrogated for a time. The whole fabric of society will fall into ruin at once until it can adjust itself to the new state of things. There will be war all over the world; crime will cover England like a cloud . . ." His voice faltered as the terrible picture grew in his brain. Both of them felt that mere words were utterly unable to express the horrors which they saw dawning.'

Here we have a new aspect of the historical phenomenon represented by this book and its popularity. Some of its attitudes to class, to sex and to the Jews offer a preview of assumptions which are to recur in popular British literature during subsequent decades. To that extent the modern reader may feel that the Edwardians were not after all so different from himself as he may have supposed. But it is impossible to imagine a novelist of any period after 1914 basing his entire plot on the assumption that a general belief in the Incarnation and the Resurrection is the sole force which prevents Western civilization from blowing up with a bang. (It was the view, one may recall, of Ivan Karamazov.) I have just used the phrase 'after 1914'. But it is really impossible to know at precisely what point in British history such a plot would cease to be credible. Naturally at the time of its publication the book was greeted with derision and occasional disgust by considerable numbers of people. But as its circulation-figures, not to mention the sermons of the bishops, show, the notion of Christianity and the literal truth of the Gospels as the main if not the sole factor holding civilization together was accepted in England to an extent which seems suddenly to remove the Edwardians to a remote and almost wholly alien world. A world which has seemed largely familiar abruptly becomes as strange as the world of the Middle Ages. This kind of illumination, this kind of jolt to one's historical sense, is among the reasons why a study of the best-sellers is of serious importance and certainly not to be considered in the light of a mere amusement to be enjoyed chiefly for the purpose of noting how 'odd' or unsophisticated their authors and mass public must have been.

What has, of course, happened is that Hands, guided by corrupt Ionides, has found the inscription forged by Sir Robert Llwellyn, and has sent the incontrovertible (so it seems) tidings to Spence. Although there was, in those days, no Press Council, Ommaney has a proper sense of journalistic responsibility and, before publishing anything, insists on a meeting with the Prime Minister. Kaiser Wilhelm, German Emperor, is also immediately made aware of the perils now facing civilization.

What is decided is that a Commission of Experts (and here we seem to be in more or less modern times) shall visit the scene. And who leads this great international Commission? None other, naturally, than Professor and Knight Llwellyn. He has no difficulty in convincing his colleagues, plus Harold Spence, who has been rushed by the *Daily Wire* to the scene, that the fatal inscription is indeed genuine. It stands up to every test.

Now it emerges that the principal, if not the only force, which has been holding civilization together is the belief that Christ rose from the dead.

Just for a start, the Turks begin to massacre the Balkan peoples. The Russians mobilize. India revolts. 'In America,' says a newspaper report,

'we find a wave of lawlessness and fierce riot passing over the country such as it has never known before. The Irishmen and the Italians who throng the congested quarters of the great cities are robbing and murdering Protestants and Jews. From Australia the foremost prelate of a great country writes of the utter overthrow of a communal moral sense . . . "Everywhere I see morals, no less than the religion which inculcates them, falling into neglect. Set aside in a spirit of despair by fathers and mothers, treated with contempt by youths and maidens, spat upon and cursed by a degraded populace, assailed with eager sarcasm by the polite and cultured."

The terrible seriousness of the situation need hardly be further insisted on here. Its reality cannot be more vividly indicated than by the statement of a single fact – C O N S O L S A R E D O W N T O S I X T Y - F I V E.'

The statement also vividly enough indicates the values and attitude of a society in which it can be published, in what the Bishop of London could describe as a 'remarkable work of fiction', and regarded as credible and at least worthy of serious discussion by scores of thousands of readers. (Hands, reading all this and regarding himself as responsible for the original 'discovery', goes partly mad and dies in a fit.)

The most significant feature of the whole affair is the effect upon the position of women. For it turns out that male belief in the Resurrection is the only factor which prevents most men treating most women in bestial fashion. In the aftermath of the news from Jerusalem, criminal assaults upon women in England rose by nearly two hundred per cent. In Ireland, 'with the exception of Ulster, the increase was only eight per cent.' The explanation for this is that at the outset the Vatican not only denied the slightest validity to the 'discovery' but absolutely forbade Roman Catholics even to discuss it. That was why the women of Southern Ireland were relatively safe, while in the Protestant North men went hog-wild.

The Secretary of the World's Women League reports that 'crimes of ordinary violence, wife-beating and the like, have increased, on an average, fifty per cent all over the United Kingdom.' He is able to produce field reports from reliable individuals up and down the country. The vicar of St Saviour's, Birmingham, notes: 'Now that the Incarnation is on all hands said to be a myth, the greatest restraint upon human passion is removed . . . In my district I have found that the moment men give up Christ and believe in this "discovery", the moment the Virgin Birth and the manifestation to the Magdalene are dismissed as untrue, women's claims to consideration and reverence for women's chastity in the eyes of these men disappear.'

Information reaching the World's Women League from the United States is no less alarming. Reclaimed prostitutes are rushing from the League's 'homes' back to the streets, only to return a few weeks later as mere wrecks, on account of the novel and appalling brutality of the men. 'The state of the lower parts of Chicago and New York City has become so bad that even the municipal authorities have become seriously alarmed. Unmentionable orgies take place in public. Accordingly a bill is to be rushed through Congress licensing so many houses of ill-fame in each city ward, according to the Continental system.'

But God is not mocked. Vengeance is mine saith the Lord. Vengeance in this case takes the form of our man Basil Gortre, curate. Gortre has all along, as we know, had his suspicions of the almost universally respected, if sometimes feared, Constantine Schuabe. Then there was the episode of the broken Murillo. And immediately after that came Schuabe's arrogantly overconfident hints of something terrible about to happen to the pale Nazarene.

Since then clues have been piling up, more particularly in an episode at Dieppe in which Gortre, on a brief holiday with Helena, Byars, and Spence, sees Llwellyn getting into the same Paris-bound express as Schuabe himself. Then occurs an amazing stroke of luck for the righteous or, it might be more prudent to say, an act of Providence. For none other than Gertrude Hunt, somewhat under the influence of the news that she is suffering from a slow complaint and has only a couple of years to live, has, to put it coarsely, 'got religion'.

Gortre's vicar at the great Bloomsbury Church of St Mary's tells him the story.

'This poor girl told me all about it, the same very sordid story one is always hearing. She is a favourite burlesque actress, and she lives very expensively in those gorgeous new flats – Bloomsbury Court. Some wealthy scoundrel pays for it all . . . Oh, my dear fellow, if the world only knew what I know! Great and honoured names in the senate, the forum, the Court, unsullied before the eyes of men. And then these hideous establishments and secret ties! This is a wicked city . . . She has expressed a wish to see you to talk things over . . . Go to her and save her. *We must . . .*'

Gortre goes to see Gertrude. He has been there only a short time when Professor Llwellyn enters. (This is just after his first, secret trip to Palestine when he forged the inscription.) Enraged at finding the young curate closeted with his Circe, he allows himself, like Schuabe on that earlier occasion, to be provoked into an astoundingly indiscreet series of threats and prophecies as to what will soon befall 'all meddling priests . . . Your Christ, your God, the pale dreamer of the East, shall be revealed to you and all men at last!'

Since that day, Gortre has secured the very useful backing of Sir Michael Manichoe, a man of colossal wealth who 'represented the curious spectacle to sociologists and the world at large, of a Jew by origin who had become a Christian by conviction and one of the sincerest sons of the English Church as he understood it . . . He had been Home Secretary under a former Conservative administration, but had retired from office.' But although now a back bencher 'he enjoyed the confidence of the chiefs of his party.'

With the help of Manichoe's money, and his own vigorous London vicar (who gets a lot of money from Manichoe to keep the church and parish going), Gortre gives Gertrude a healthy Christian brain-washing, and gets her secretly to disappear from Bloomsbury Court Mansions and the clutches of Sir Robert Llwellyn. She goes into concealment in a remote country village.

Meanwhile Sir Robert, what with over-rich food and nervous

premonitions brought on by the crash of civilization he has helped to bring about, is a prey to overpowering sexual lust for the absconding Gertrude. Nobody else will satisfy him. Gortre in London and Gertrude in her hide-out sense this. After much soul-searching, they decide that, horrible and in some senses sinful as such a course must be, the right thing for her to do is to return to Sir Robert, play upon his lusts, and worm out of him the truth of what Gortre knows must be the case, but can produce no evidence to prove.

She does so. In a passionate bedroom scene Llwellyn tells all, boastfully and in detail.

Gertrude hurries off to report.

Ommaney and Harold Spence are now at once brought into action. Spence is sent off to Palestine with unlimited money. He runs to earth Ionides, who, just after Llwellyn's first visit, has 'inherited' a large sum of money and retired to a country village a couple of days ride from Jerusalem.

Spence, after paying over a heavy bribe to the Turkish Governor of the area, secures a tough bodyguard and goes out to Ionides' house. The Turkish official has asked, and secured from a slightly reluctant Spence, permission to torture Ionides if that is the only way to secure his confession.

The threat is sufficient. Ionides tells how he was bribed to assist Llwellyn in the faking of the alleged message from Joseph of Arimathea, the re-sealing and its subsequent discovery by Hands, led thither by Ionides.

With this confession, the fate of Schuabe, the Professor and their whole conspiracy is sealed. Not only the establishment but the deluded populace turn against them. Llwellyn is lynched, trampled to death by the mob under the eyes of his wife in the home which he has so often deserted.

Schuabe escapes to Manchester with the intention of committing suicide. He fails and goes mad. He is taken to the County Asylum.

It was apparently customary, or at least not unusual, at that time for visitors to be shown round the asylum as an alternative to visiting, for instance, the Zoo. One afternoon the chaplain was showing a group of young ladies over the place. The girls were three in number, young and fashionably dressed. They talked without ceasing in an empty-headed stream of girlish chatter. They were the daughters of a great iron founder in the district and would each have a hundred thousand pounds.

'How sweet of you, Mr Pritchard!' said one of the girls, 'to show us everything. It's awfully thrilling.'

The party 'went laughing through the long spotless corridors, peeping into the bright, airy living rooms where bodies without brains were mumbling and singing to each other.'

' "Did ye show the young ladies Schuabe?" said the doctor to the chaplain.

"Bless my soul!" he replied, "I must be going mad myself. I'd almost forgotten to show you Schuabe!"

"Who is Schuabe?" said the youngest of the sisters, a girl just fresh from school at St Leonards.

"Oh Maisie!" said the eldest. "Surely you remember . . . He was the Manchester millionaire who went mad after trying to blow up the tomb of Christ. I think that was it. It was in all the papers. A young clergyman found out what he had been trying to do . . ."

"Everyone likes to have a look at this patient," said the doctor. "He has a little sleeping room of his own and a special attendant. His money was all confiscated by the Government, but they allow two hundred a year for him. Otherwise he would be among the paupers."

The girls giggled with pleasurable anticipation. The doctor unlocked a door. The party entered a fairly large room, simply furnished . . . On a bed lay the idiot. He had grown very fat and looked healthy. The features were all coarsened, but the hair retained its colour of dark red. He was sleeping.

"Now, Miss Clegg, ye'd never think that made such a stir in the world but five years since. But there he lies. He always eats as much as he can, and goes to sleep after the meal."

"He's waking up now, sir. Here, Mr Schuabe, some ladies have come to see you."

It got up with a foolish grin and began some ungainly capers.

"Thank you so much, Mr Pritchard," the girls said as they left the building. "We've enjoyed ourselves *so* much."

"I like the little man with his tongue hanging out the best," said one.

"Oh Mabel, you've no sense of humour. That Schuabe creature was the funniest of all." '

And thus, with the blessing of the Bishops of London and Exeter, we leave a book highly recommended by them to the British public and by that public enthusiastically received.

There is, I suppose, a difference between those rich girls giggling so heartily at the lunatics, and the hangers and torturers of our own day. The differences are indeed obvious and can be studied in laws and by-laws. Perhaps still more interesting to study would be the similarities, not always obvious, between our own times and the days when it was dark.

The oblong blur

'As Domini leaned out, seeing nothing, she was conscious
that in this breath she drank, there was a soul, and it seemed
to her a soul that flames in the centre of things and beyond . . .
All religions were surely here, marching side by side; and
behind them, background to them, there was something far
greater than any religion. Was it snow or fire? Was it the
lawlessness of that which has made laws, or the calm of that
which has brought passion into being? Greater love than is
in any creed or greater freedom that is in any human liberty?'

The sentiments here expressed by Miss Domini Enfilden in an
African train *en route* for the Sahara would have been repugnant
indeed to Basil Gortre, curate, and hero of *When It Was
Dark*. His views it will be remembered, were very far from
ecumenical. His reverence for the High Church was accompanied
by an almost savage hatred and contempt for those following
other trends in the Church of England, let alone Methodists,
Wesleyans, nonconformists of all kinds, and of course Jews. He
does indicate a certain admiration for the authoritarianism of the
Roman Catholic Church. But stuff about 'all religions' being
'surely here, marching side by side' expressed just the kind of
attitude which his author denounced and combated and derided
in *When It Was Dark*. To his mind, it was the kind of attitude,
mushy and liberal, which was largely responsible for the fact
that the sinister Schuabe and Professor Llwellyn were able to
succeed temporarily in their plot. True Anglicans of the better
sort would not have believed that the story of the Resurrection
was false even in the face of all the scientific evidence in the
world. As for this business of 'snow or fire' and so on, it was
sheer paganism. Yet here we have this mishmash of anarchic ideas
dripping, apparently quite naturally, through the mind of this
rich young Englishwoman, daughter of the late Lord Rens. At

the moment she is confronted with the landscape of North Africa.
Moreover she is the heroine of a novel, *The Garden of Allah*,
by Robert Hichens, which is going to be published in the year
after *When It Was Dark*, and is ultimately going to outsell it
hugely. That she is the daughter of a Lord, and rich, would
make her all the more menacing in the eyes of Basil Gortre.
Nor would it have been much comfort to him to know that
she is a steadfast Roman Catholic and is going to remain so to
the end.

To the modern reader, even though he may happen to belong
to some Christian sect, the steamy religiosity of *The Garden of
Allah* can come as a shock. Its rich odours may seem exotic —
a pong from far away. Can it really be, he may ask, that this
was the kind of hot cakes which sold best in 1904 and subsequent years? The short answer is of course that it can be
because it certainly was so. But this supra-ecumenical theme
recurs, as we shall see, in many different forms throughout the
subsequent decades. For a bestseller, God was a useful though
not entirely indispensable asset. (I do not intend to imply that
the authors who brought on God in a major or minor role were
cynically exploiting the religiosity of the British public. They
were simply in tune with the public.) But the readership included
members of many Christian sects. Even as early as 1904 it
included, too, a by no means negligible percentage of people
who, while declining allegiance to any particular creed, or even
showing hostility to any form of organized religion, would state
that they believed in a Higher Power, a Spiritual something
which must exist because otherwise what was the meaning of
Life? Their position was roughly that of the American clergyman who, when asked what was his view of God, replied that
he always thought of him as 'a kind of oblong blur'. The concept
of the oblong blur obviously appealed to that tolerant broad-
mindedness upon which members of the British middle class
sometimes rightly, sometimes wrongly, prided themselves. It was
a way of leaving all religious options open. The passage quoted,
which occurs very early in the book, certainly does that. At
irregular intervals in this enormously long novel Hichens seems
to be suggesting that there is not much to choose between the
God of the Christians and the Allah of the Moslems and that,
in some vaguely pantheistic universe, the desert itself, the

Sahara, embodies and exercises supernatural powers. So far so clear. It is all a natural part of that oblong blur, with tints of *couleur de rose* which so many Edwardians evidently liked to have hovering around their fiction. It is to be sighted often enough in a best-seller due to appear a few years later, namely, de Vere Stacpoole's *The Blue Lagoon*. Superficially it is obvious that the Edwardians found in this kind of thing an assurance that their popular fiction, derided as trivial, shoddy, and escapist by some, was in reality dealing with the most serious possible ideas, was continuously striking a deeper note. *The Garden of Allah* almost certainly offered material for 'serious' discussion to far more people than any play of Bernard Shaw. To that extent religiosity simply made the popular novel more socially and in a sense intellectually respectable.

But one might well judge from books of this kind and the public reaction to them that the appeal of religiosity went rather deeper than that. It used to be imagined – still is by many people – that the Edwardians, with the scare and frights of the Boer War behind them and a boom on the markets only briefly interrupted by the American panic of 1907, can have been in no need of distraction from nervous scares of things to come. The editor of the *Encyclopaedia Britannica*, writing in 1910 for the eleventh edition, does seem to have been one of those who justified charges of complacency brought against people of his generation. Concluding his survey of British history up to the accession of George V he wrote :

'The new king succeeded to a noble heritage. The monarchy itself was popular, the country was prosperous and in good relations with the world, except for the increasing naval rivalry with Germany, and the consciousness of imperial solidarity had made extraordinary progress among all the dominions. However the domestic problems in the United Kingdom might be solved, the future of the greatness of the English throne lay with its headship of an empire, loyal to the core, over which the sun never sets.'

Certainly there must have been a great many people who believed that kind of thing. There were a great many more who wished to believe it and repeated such stuff like an incantation, a spell to avert suspected evil. To judge by the newspaper files there was a large majority of people who, on the contrary, worried. One may say that it is unreasonable to judge by the newspaper files. The newspapers, particularly the Northcliffe Press, had a vested interest in the manufacture of 'scares', particularly war scares. They purported to be performing a patriotic duty in stirring the sluggish British public from its state of dangerous apathy. But Lord Northcliffe and his fellows were not philanthropists. If 'scares' of one kind and another had not helped to sell newspapers he would have devoted less space to them. Scare stories sold newspapers because they appealed to a deep and continuing uneasiness in the public mind. The *Encyclopaedia Britannica* almost blithely declared the British Empire to be all right, 'however the domestic problems in the United Kingdom might be solved'. This offhand treatment of the 'domestic problems' was not shared by large sections of the middle class. Many of that class thought, in terror or resignation, that the likeliest solution of those domestic problems, in the coal fields and on the railways for instance, was revolution. Certainly it is true to say that even the most worried worriers did not worry all the time about the attitude of the miners, the railwaymen, the Kaiser, or even the Chancellor of the Exchequer. It would be an absurd over-simplification of the definition of man as a 'political animal' to suppose that they did. But in the 'private sector', the field of 'personal relations', there was plenty to bother them as well. It would be convenient simply to state that during this period England was passing through a moral crisis. Convenient, but perhaps unhelpful, since it may be claimed with some justification that there has never been a period during which a moral crisis was not being passed through. It probably has to be recognized that some crises are more critical than others. One may cite the crises detected by historians in the aftermath of each World War. Looking back at the Edwardians, people of our own day might be inclined to remember what the Red Queen said to Alice. Alice had referred to 'that hill'. 'When you say "hill",' the Queen interrupted, 'I could show you hills, in comparison with which you'd call that a valley.'

A moral crisis is very much what you think it is. It could even be argued that if you think you are passing through a grave moral crisis, that is what you are doing. In any case you have no possibility of measuring it against the moral crises which are going to occur in the future. Everyone has heard so often that the words slither across the brain from one ear to the other, that this or that period was one in which 'previously accepted moral values were being gravely questioned', 'the foundations of previously accepted beliefs were being shaken', uncertainty replaced certainty about almost every aspect of human behaviour'. But by becoming platitudinous a statement does not necessarily cease to be at least partially true. The foundations of what is called in shorthand the Victorian Age had been shaking for a long time before Edward VII came to the throne. The insane virulence of the reaction to the Wilde trial, the violence of that particular backlash, disclosed profound uncertainties and apprehensions in the mind of the middle class. Much the same may be said about the widespread hostility and fear occasioned by the plays of, for instance, Bernard Shaw. No writer can raise flourishing plants from seed unless the soil, however apparently unpromising, contains elements nutritious for that particular seed. Certainly for a long time Shaw's plays and ideas had more enemies than friends. As happens when a writer makes that kind of impact, the plays were attacked by greater numbers of people than had actually seen or read them. But this inevitable type of public reaction is in itself a proof of the instability, at a given period, of hitherto accepted ideas and of supposedly immutable 'moral values', etc. In other words, however calm and easily navigable the waters of Edwardian life may have been made to appear by later commentators, to those making the crossing the sea seemed to be at the best choppy and at the worst surging with enormous billows driven by winds from unknown or sinister quarters, threatening at any moment to poop the vessel. I am not saying that everyone felt that way. I am saying that enough people did so to determine certain characteristics of the popular novel.

The creator of the potential best-seller, the good physician, could approach his patients and their malaises in various ways. (The statement is not intended to mean that the novelist always or perhaps ever thought of his works in terms of a kind of social therapy.) One method is represented by the romantic historian and historical novelist. It is to this *genre* that the term 'escapism' most accurately applies. In this field of work Jeffery Farnol was a master. De Vere Stacpoole's *The Blue Lagoon* would certainly be called 'escapist' in the sense that its setting is a world totally in contrast to the world familiar to the reader. But bathed in the moonshine of that world, the characters can be said to behave more or less realistically. *The Garden of Allah* undertakes a third approach to the problem. The deeper note is struck almost at the outset. Every reader can see that he is in for a serious read with grave matters gravely handled. God, first in the form of the 'oblong blur' and later in a very much more precise form, broods heavily over the narrative. Moral problems with particular reference to love and sex are posed with the repetitive insistence of a tomtom, but a tomtom which is not merely insistent but is seeking to convey a lesson of profound significance.

A modern reader might find it heavy going. There are *longueurs*. There are passages in which Hichens' vehicle seems to be pushing its way through the sand on deflated tyres. At the same time the totality of the book is finely constructed, the suspense and the impression conveyed that the matters in suspense will turn out to be of real concern are continuously sustained.

We first encounter Domini Enfilden in bed in an hotel in a North African port reading Newman's *The Dream of Gerontius*. She interrupts herself to open the window and look out at the African night.

'As she stood there face to face with a wonder that she could not see, Domini forgot Newman. She felt the brave companionship of mystery. In it she divined the beating pulses, the hot surging blood of freedom.

She wanted freedom, a wide horizon, the great winds, the great sun, the terrible spaces, the glowing, shimmering radiance, the hot, entrancing noons and bloomy purple nights of Africa. She wanted the nomad's fires and the acid voices of the Kabyle dogs. She wanted the roar of the tom-toms, the clash of the cymbals, the rattle of the negroes' castanets, the fluttering painted fingers of the dancers. She wanted – more than she could express, more than she knew. It was there, want aching in her heart, as she drew into her nostrils this strange and wealthy atmosphere.

When Domini returned to her bed she found it impossible to read any more Newman.'

On her train journey to the interior she shares a carriage with a bizarre fellow traveller. He behaves boorishly at first and then aloofly, but something peculiar about him engages Domini's interest. Indeed she has a kind of waking dream there in the carriage in which she finds herself staring at a face 'like a face looking out of the heart of the sun . . . and she knew that she was staring into the face of the man who had behaved so rudely at the station of El-Akdara.'

His physical appearance is minutely described and much of it must surely provide a hidden clue to his mysterious identity. Thus

'he moved his hands uneasily. Domini noticed that they scarcely tallied with his face. Though scrupulously clean, they looked like the hands of a labourer, hard, broad, and brown. Even his wrists, and a small section of his left forearm, which showed as he lifted his left hand from one knee to the other, were heavily tinted by the sun. The spaces between the fingers were wide, as they usually are in hands accustomed to grasping implements, but the fingers themselves were rather delicate and artistic . . . the hand looked violent . . . despite the glory of the sunset on him there seemed to be a cold shadow in his eyes. The faint lines near his mouth looked deeper than before, and now suggested more powerfully the dreariness, the harshness of long continued suffering. The mouth itself was compressed and grim and the man's whole expression was fierce and startling as the expression of a criminal bracing himself to endure inevitable detection. So cold and piercing indeed was this mouth confronting her that Domini started and was inclined to shudder. For a minute the man's eyes held hers and she thought she saw in them unfathomable depths of misery or of wickedness. She hardly knew which. Sorrow was like crime, and crime like the sheer desolation of grief to her just then. And she thought of the outer darkness spoken of in the Bible. It came before her in the sunset . . . The thing was as vital, and fled as swiftly as a hallucination in the madman's brain . . . there was a black spot on the sun – humanity, God's mistake in the great plan of Creation. And the shadow cast by humanity entered, even surely conquered the light. She wondered if she would always feel the cold of the sunless places in the golden dominion of the sun.'

On arrival at their common destination, the small town of

Beni-Mora, a significant thing happens. Domini sees the stranger
walking ahead of her on the path leading directly to the hotel.
Suddenly he pauses in his 'curious shuffling stride', hesitates,
stares fixedly ahead of him, then turns abruptly on to another
path leading directly away from the hotel. What he has seen
approaching is a priest in a soutane. 'Her attention was beginning
to be strongly fixed upon the unknown man. His appearance and
manner were so unusual that it was impossible not to notice
him.'

His extreme aversion to priests and all that goes with them
becomes more marked in the days that follow. Domini observes
him from the wall which, at the edge of the desert, encloses the
beautifully cultivated property of Count Anteoni. Domini has
not been introduced to the Count and 'the timbre of his voice
was harsh and grating, yet it was a very interesting, even a
seductive, voice and, Domini thought, peculiarly full of vivid
life, though not of energy. His manner at once banished her
momentary discomfort. There is a freemasonry between people
born in the same social world. By the way in which Count
Anteoni took off his hat and spoke she knew at once that all was
right.'

The Count is an expatriate aesthetic with a lot of philosophy
of life. He speaks a good deal of Truth and of Peace and above
all of the desert.

From the wall the Count and Domini peer through field-
glasses at two figures espied in the distance under some palm
trees. One is a tall one-eyed Arab, the other is the mysterious
stranger of the train. At this moment the Muezzin gives the call
to prayer.

'The tall Arab under the palm sank down swiftly. Domini
kept the glasses at her eyes. Through them, as in a sort of
exaggerated vision, very far off, yet intensely distinct, she saw
the man with whom she had travelled in the train. He went
to and fro, to and fro on the burning ground till the fourth
call of the Muezzin died away. Then, as he approached the
isolated palm tree and saw the Arab beneath it fall to the
earth and bow his long body in prayer, he paused and stood
still as if in contemplation. The glasses were so powerful
that it was possible to see the expressions on faces even at
that distance. The expression on the traveller's face was, or

seemed to be, at first one of profound attention. But this changed swiftly as he watched the bowing figure, and was succeeded by a look of uneasiness, then of fierce disgust, then – surely – of fear or horror. He turned sharply away like a driven man, and hurried off along the cliff edge in his striding walk, quickening his steps each moment till his departure became a flight.

Domini laid the glasses down on the wall and looked at Count Anteoni.

"You say an atheist in the desert is unimaginable?"

"Isn't it true?"

"Has an atheist a hatred, a horror of prayer?"

"Chi lo sa? The devil shrank away from the lifted Cross."

"Because he knew how much that was true it symbolised."

"No doubt had it been otherwise he would have jeered, not cowered. But why do you ask me this question, Madame?"

"I have just seen a man flee from the sight of prayer."

"Your fellow traveller?"

"Yes. It was horrible."

She gave him back the glasses. "They reveal that which should be hidden," she said.

Count Anteoni took the glasses slowly from her hands. As he bent to do it he looked steadily at her, and she could not read the expression in his eyes.

"The desert is full of truth. Is that what you mean?" he asked.

She made no reply. Count Anteoni stretched out his hand to the shining expanse before them.

"The man who is afraid of prayer is unwise to set foot beyond the palm trees," he said.

"Why unwise?"

He answered her very gravely. "The Arabs have a saying: 'The desert is the garden of Allah'." '

In the hotel restaurant a little later she notices a table set for one.

'As she glanced at the empty chair standing before the knives and forks, and the white cloth, she was uncertain whether she wished it to be filled by the traveller or not. She felt his presence in Beni-Mora as a warring element. That she

knew . . . In the presence of this total stranger there was something unpleasantly distracting which she could not and did
not ignore, something which roused her antagonism and which
at the same time compelled her attention . . . He was there
like an enemy, like something determined, egoistical, that said
to her, "you would look at the greatness of the desert, at im-
mensity, infinity, God! — look at me." And she could not turn
her eyes away. Each time the man had, as if without effort,
conquered the great competing power, fastened her thoughts
upon himself, set her imagination working about his life, even
made her heart beat faster with some thrill of — what? Was it
pity? Was it a faint horror? She knew that to call the feeling
merely repugnance would not be sincere. The intensity, the
vitality of the force shut up in the human being almost angered
her at this moment as she looked at the empty chair and realised all that had suddenly set to work. There was something
insolent in humanity as well as something divine, and just then
she felt the insolence more than the divinity.'

The love-hate relationship between Domini and the stranger,
who turns out to be half Russian and to be called Androvsky,
develops at a fast clip. This development is urged along its way
by the physical and emotional atmospherics of Beni-Mora. The
sunrises, sunsets, and storms are alike glorious or lurid, evocative
of mental peace or turmoil. The Count continues to philosophize
on the meaning of life. Arab dancers, in a longish sequence, also
evoke strange visions and sensations in the spectators, notably
Domini and Androvsky. The Count lays on a Diviner who,
by gazing into sand, foresees the immediate future of Domini and
Another. Comes the day when Androvsky and Domini are to be
married and undertake together that journey south across the
desert which Domini had intended from the beginning. On the
day of the wedding the weather co-operates, to emphasize that
this is no ordinary ceremony.

'The dawn came struggling like an exhausted pilgrim
through the windy dark, pale and faint, with no courage, it
seemed, to grow bravely into day. As if with faint and sedulous
effort of something weary but of unconquered will, it
slowly lit up Beni-Mora with a feeble light that flickered in a
cloud of whirling sand, revealing the desolation of an almost

featureless void. The village, the whole oasis, was penetrated by a passionate fog that instead of brooding heavily, phlegmatically, over the face of life and nature travelled like a demented thing bent upon instant destruction and coming thus cloudily to be free for crime. It was an emissary of the desert, propelled with irresistible force from the furthest recesses of the dunes, and the desert itself seemed to be hurrying behind it as if to spy upon the doings of its deeds. As the sea in a great storm rages against the land, ferocious that land should be, so the desert now raged against the oasis that ventured to exist in its bosom. Every palm tree was the victim of its wrath, every running rill, every habitation of man . . .

Everywhere in the oasis it came with a lust to kill, but surely its deepest enmity was concentrated upon the Catholic church.'

Father Roubier, the local priest, has all along been filled with a nameless horror of Androvsky. For no explicit reason except the man's sinister hostility to priests, Father Roubier senses in him a force opposed to religion and to God – he sees him almost as anti-Christ. He feels that even to perform the marriage ceremony is somehow an outrageous act.

'Yet how could he help performing this act – he knew that he would do it. Within a few minutes he would be standing before the altar, he would be looking into the faces of this man and woman whose love he was called upon to consecrate. He would consecrate it and they would go out from him into the desert, man and wife.

His eyes fell upon a silver crucifix that was hanging upon the wall in front of him. He was not a very imaginative man, not a man given to fancies, a dreamer of dreams more real to him than life or a seer of visions. But today he was stirred, and perhaps the unwonted turmoil of his mind acted subtlely upon his nervous system. Afterwards he felt certain that it must have been so for in no other way could he account for a fantasy that beset him at this moment.

As he looked at the crucifix there came against the church a more furious beating of the wind, and it seemed to him that Christ upon the Cross shuddered.

He saw it shudder. He started, leaned across the table and

stared at the crucifix with eyes that were fuller with amazement than with horror . . . he knew that for the first time in his
life he had been the slave of an optical delusion. He knew it,
and yet he could not banish the feeling that God Himself was
averse from the act that he was on the point of committing in
this church that confronted Islam, that God Himself shuddered
as surely even He, the Creator, must shudder at some of the
actions of His creatures. And this feeling added immensely to
the distress of the priest's mind . . .

   With every day his antipathy for Androvsky increased. Yet
he was entirely unable to ground it upon any definite fact in
Androvsky's character. He did not know that character. The
man was as much a mystery to him as on the day when they
first met. And to this living mystery from which his soul re-
coiled he was about to consign, with all the beautiful and
solemn blessings of his church, a woman whose character he
respected, whose innate purity, strength and nobility he had
quickly divined, and no less quickly learned to love.'

The priest's reverie is interrupted by the entry of his little
acolyte, a young French boy.

   'He began to take the priest's robes out of the cupboard.
   Just then the wind wailed again furiously about the church,
and the crucifix fell down upon the floor of the sacristy.
   The priest started forward, picked it up, and stood with it
in his hands. He glanced at the wall and saw at once that the
nail to which the crucifix had been fastened had come out of
its hole. A flake of the plaster had been detached perhaps
some days ago and the hole had become too large to retain the
nail. The explanation of the matter was perfectly simple and
comprehensible. Yet the priest felt as if a catastrophe had just
taken place. As he stared at the cross he heard a little noise
near him. The acolyte was crying.
   "Why, Paul, what's the matter?" he said.
   "Why did it do that?" exclaimed the boy, as if alarmed.
"Why did it do that?"
   "Perhaps it was the wind. Everything is shaking." '

Those who in 1903 had followed the advice of the Bishop of
London and read carefully Guy Thorne's *When It Was Dark*

4
Erskine Childers
Radio Times
Hulton Picture
Library

5
Ian Hay
Radio Times
Hulton Picture
Library

6
Jeffery Farnol
*Radio Times Hulton
Picture Library*

7
Warwick Deeping
Cassell and Company Limited

8
A. S. M. Hutchinson
Bassano and Vandyk

must certainly have recalled as they reached this passage about
halfway through *The Garden of Allah* the scene in which, just
as the maid announced the arrival of Schuabe to call on the vicar,
the curate Gortre made a sudden movement and knocked from
the marble mantelshelf 'a head of Christ, photographed on china,
from Murillo . . . and dislodged the picture which fell upon the
floor and was broken into a hundred pieces, crashing loudly
upon the fender.' The strangely parallel scenes in *When It Was
Dark* and *The Garden of Allah* have a singular interest. To appre-
ciate them one need only reflect on the improbability of any
author of our day, however religious his theme, introducing such
episodes into a novel. There is no way that I can think of to pin-
point the precise date at which to do so would have incurred the
ridicule of most readers and the contempt of other authors outraged by the use of so crude a device. The fact remains that the
device was still in Hichens' day not merely acceptable but impressive; otherwise why should this have been used twice in a
single year by two such skilled craftsmen as Thorne and Hichens?
We cannot say that devices similarly crude, hocus-pocus equally
murky are not used by novelists, and impressive to readers, in the
1970s. We can only say that the particular kind of hocus-pocus
exemplified by the story of the photograph and the crucifix was
attractive to the Edwardian.

The married couple journey southwards into the desert and have
a great deal of weather, and highly charged conversations. The
darkness has already fallen on the first day of their married life
when they at length enter their tent.

'A stronger gust of the night wind followed them. Androvsky
took his arm slowly from Domini and turned to let down the
flap of the tent. While he was doing this she stood quite still.
The flame of the lamp flickered, throwing its light now here
now there uneasy. She saw the cross [she has brought one with
her] lit up for an instant and the white bed beneath. The wind
stirred her dark hair and she was cold about her neck. In
that brief moment while Androvsky was fastening the tent she
lived through centuries of intensive complicated emotion. When
the light flickered over the cross she felt as if she could spend
her life in passionate adoration at its foot: but when she did
not see it, and the wind coming in from the desert from the

tent door where she heard the movement of Androvsky stirred in her hair, she felt reckless, wayward, savage – and something more. A cry rose in her that was like the cry of a stranger who was of her and in her and from whom she would not part.

Again the lamplight flickered upon the cross. Quickly while she saw the cross plainly, she went forward to the bed and fell on her knees by it, bending down her face upon its whiteness.

When Androvsky had fastened the tent door, he turned round and saw her kneeling. He stood quite still as if petrified, staring at her. Then, as the flame, now sheltered from the wind, burned steadily he saw the cross. He started as if someone had struck him, hesitated, then, with a look of fierce and concentrated resolution on his face, went to the cross, pulled it from the canvas. He held it in his hand for an instant, then moved to the tent door and stood to unfasten the cord that held it to the pegs with the intention of throwing the cross out into the night. But he did not unfasten the cord. Something – some sudden change of feeling, some secret and powerful reluctance – checked him. He thrust the cross into his pocket. Then, returning to where Domini was kneeling, he put his arms round her and drew her to him.

She did not resist him. Still holding her in his arms he blew out the lamp.'

For three weeks they travelled across the desert. 'They had become as one with the nomads whose home is the moving tent, whose hearthstone is the yellow sand of the dunes, whose God is liberty.' Then a series of human encounters, notably with a French officer and a priest, precipitate a new situation. At this point the role of, as it were, *diabolus ex machina* is performed by a liqueur. It is called Louarine and the Androvskys happen to have a flask or two of it with them. A priest who is visiting Domini in the camp starts and exclaims at the sight of it. Finally he tells Domini its story. It comes from the Trappist monastery of El-Largani near Tunis;

' "they grow every sort of thing but their vineyards are specially famous and their wines bring in a splendid revenue. This is their only liqueur, this Louarine. It too has brought in a lot of money to the community but when what they have in stock at the monastery now is exhausted, they will never make another Louarine. The secret of its manufacture belonged to one monk only. At his death he was to confide it to another whom he had chosen."

"And he died suddenly without – "

"Madame, he didn't die."

The gravity had returned to the priest's face and deepened there, transforming it. He put the glass down without touching his lips.

"Then – I don't understand."

"He disappeared from the monastery."

"Do you mean he left it – a Trappist?"

"Yes."

"After taking the final vows?"

"Oh, he had been a monk at El-Largani for over twenty years."

"How horrible!" Domini said. She looked at the pale green liquid. "How horrible!" she repeated.

. . . "After twenty years, to go!" she added after a moment. "And there was no reason – no excuse – no, I don't mean excuse! but had nothing exceptional happened?"

"What exceptional thing can happen in a Trappist monastery?" said the priest. "One day is exactly like another, one year exactly like another."

"Was it long ago?"

"No, not very long ago, only some months. Oh, perhaps it may be a year by now but not more. Poor fellow! I suppose he was a man who didn't know himself, Madame, and the devil tempted him."

"But after twenty years!" said Domini.

The thing to her seemed almost incredible.

"That man must be in hell now," she added. "In the hell a man can make for himself by his own act. Oh, here is my husband." '

Domini naturally recounts the story to Androvsky, not concealing an incredulous horror at the impious act of the delinquent Trappist. There follow some rather long hours of emotional disturbance. Androvsky, in a fever, is seen all too clearly to be harbouring some secret grief. Count Anteoni drops in to announce that he is to become a Mohammedan. Domini perceives that it has made him happy. 'His eyes had always held a shadow.

Now that shadow was lifted out of them. How deep was the
shadow in her husband's eyes. How deep it had been in the eyes
of her father. He had died with a terrible darkness in his eyes and
in his soul. If her husband were to die thus! Terror came upon
her. She looked out at the stones and the sand and imagined
herself there – as the old Arab was – praying for Androvsky
buried there, hidden from her on earth for ever. And suddenly
she felt, "I cannot wait, I must act." '

She pleads with him to unburden himself, to share his secret
sorrow with her. At length he tells her that he has asked the
local priest to hear his confession, but has been unable to bring
himself to make it.

' "I can only make it to you, Domini – only to you. Do you
hear, Domini? You want to know what it is makes me unhappy even in our love – desperately unhappy. It is this. I believe in God, I love God, and I have consulted Him. I tried to
forget God, to deny Him, put human love higher than love for
Him, but always I am haunted by the thought of God, that
thought makes my despair. Once when I was young, I gave
myself to God. I have broken the vows I made, I have – I
have – "

The hardness went out of his voice. He broke down for a
moment, silent.

"You gave yourself to God?" she said. "How?"

He tried to meet her questioning eyes but he could not.

"I – I gave myself to God as a monk," he said after a pause.

As he spoke Domini saw before her in the moonlight de
Trevignac [a French officer who visited her in the desert]. He
cast a glance of horror at the tent, bent over her, made the sign
of the Cross and vanished. In his place stood Father Roubier,
his eyes shining, his hand upraised, warning her against
Androvsky. Then he too vanished and she seemed to see Count
Anteoni dressed as a monk and muttering words of the Koran.

"You are the Trappist," she said quietly, "of whom the
priest told me. You are the monk from the monastery of El-
Largani who disappeared after twenty years."

"Yes," he said, "I am he."

"What made you tell me? What made you tell me?" There
was agony now in her voice.'

He tells her the whole story of how he became a Trappist, how
he remained in the monastery for twenty years, and the concate-
nation of circumstances which tempted him to leave. It is a narrative which in its simplicity and restrained realism introduces an
element of genuine and credible tragedy into *The Garden of
Allah*. It is as though another writer had inserted into the book
a short story which could in fact be read independently.

After much soul-searching and mental agony Domini makes
a final decision. They are to return to Beni-Mora. There will be
no more wedded intercourse. There Androvsky is to make his
confession to Father Roubier. And then having set himself to
that extent to rights with God he is to return to the monastery of
El-Largani to fulfil his broken vow of lifelong dedication. On the
last night before his re-entry they sit together on the marble seat
of a temple overlooking Tunis.

'Androvsky was shaken by sobs.
"How can I part from you?" he said. "Why was I given
this love for you, this terrible thing crying out, reaching out
heart and soul to you? Domini, what does it all mean – this
mystery of torture, this – scourging of the body – this tearing
in pieces that my soul feels? Domini, shall we know, shall we
ever know?"

"I am sure we shall know, we shall all know some day and
then perhaps then surely we shall each of us be glad to have
suffered. You will see me in your prayers every day and I
shall see you in mine."

"The cry of the body, Domini, of the eyes, of the hands, to
see, to touch – so fierce, so – so – "

"I know, I hear it too. But there is another voice which
will be strong when the other has faded into eternal silence.
In all bodily things, even the most beautiful, there is something finite. We must reach out our poor trembling hands to
the infinite." '

In due course, Domini has given birth to Androvsky's son. They
are living in the house and garden of Count Anteoni. In the
garden the little boy plays happily. The cool wind of the night
blows over the Sahara touching her cheek, reminding her of the
wind that carried fire towards her as she sat before the tent,

reminding her of the glorious days of liberty, of the passion that
came to her soul like fire.

> 'But she does not rebel.
> For always, when night falls, she sees the form of a man
> praying who once fled from prayer. She sees a wanderer who
> at last has reached his home.'

It is impossible by summary or quotation to ram home the full
charges of sexual passion with which the book is loaded. It is
difficult to realize at this date that there were many who considered the book nearly obscene. Many years later, when *The
Sheik* appeared, and also sprang on to the bestseller lists, they
were able to make their point. They pondered the fact that the
heroine of *The Sheik*, no less well-born than Domini Enfilden
('proud Diana Mayo had the history of her race at her fingers'
ends'), was straightforwardly ravished in the open desert over and
over again, and went joyously to bed with the seemingly
black man long before he proved to be racially marriageable. God
was not dragged into the matter. This could be seen as more
wholesome than Domini's affair, in which a passion (just as
technically sinful as the old priest feared) was made respectable
for a few hot weeks by marriage, and then agonizingly damned
on religious principle, though not too soon to beget a nice child.

This could be considered a simple device for letting the gentle
reader have it both ways. But the book poses some interesting
questions about the spiritual beliefs of the English.

As has been seen, the action of the novel, the behaviour of
the characters, is religiously motivated, makes no sense without
that motivation. It would be excessively unreasonable to assume
that there were more than a few readers who regarded this religious drama in the way that they might have regarded a story
based on the religious beliefs, taboos and rituals of a primitive
tribe. But the motivation is not merely such as might be expected
to be produced by awareness of the Oblong Blur. Throughout,
the criterion of good and evil is the strict doctrine of the Roman
Catholic Church. And this was put forward in a country where
only a small minority of the population was Catholic.

A devout Roman Catholic might have no difficulty in explaining that this was no genuine paradox. Wandering bewildered
in Protestant heresies, not to mention those fallen utterly into

agnosticism or paganism, the reader must necessarily be attracted by the light of the 'true faith' in action, even though refracted through the pages of popular fiction. Or, perhaps, popular fiction might be God's way of making his mysteries plain to ordinary people. The unbeliever would have to answer rather differently. And I expect he would soon find himself forced to lay one more straw on the back of that overworked camel-word 'Alienation'. But we have to remember that the camel is overworked only because it is useful and there is no other word-of-burden which can adequately do the job.

In a work published in 1888 and entitled *An Estimate of the Value of influence of Works of Fiction in Modern Times*, T. H. Green wrote:

'In the progressive division of labour, while we become more useful as citizens, we seem to lose our completeness as men . . . the perfect organisation of modern society removes the excitement of adventure and the occasion for independent effort. There is less of human interest to touch us within our calling . . . the alleviation . . . is to be found in the newspaper and the novel.'

Hardly anyone doubts that there are many tasks, the tasks most people are compelled to perform in order to exist in that state of life which they wish to occupy, or to maintain that position in life which they do not want to lose, which can be tolerable and even exhilarating when conducted in the supposed service of some cause or objective, and become drudgery when the light of that cause or objective begins to flicker. It may be said that the great cause of making money is a sufficient common cause and common objective to keep most men going most of the time. This is only superficially true. There is much difference between the emotional state of the man on the way up, or the man who supposes he is on the way up, and dedicates himself whole-heartedly to making a fortune before he either retires or dies, and that of another man who knows, except in moments of fantasy, that he is never going to make a fortune and wants to make money simply because he wants to stay in the same place. And this second man is in a majority in our society.

To that extent he is alienated from his work. For every man who can generally be said to enjoy his work there are nineteen others who consciously or subconsciously believe that they start living when they leave their offices at the end of a week-day's employment, and when the weekend opens before them. These periods of 'real life' may be lived to the full in various ways. There are games. There is sex. There is drinking. There is conversation. And there is also reading.

In the times of, for instance, Jane Austen, the reading of novels was widely regarded as a reprehensible waste of time, certainly impermissible in the morning. The readers thus reprimanded were usually women. Their novel-reading was seen as an escape from tasks about the house and garden which ought to have been as congenial as they were useful. And it is true that to read a novel in the morning was a sign that the reader was alienated from her task of arranging the flowers or visiting the poor. It is probably true that at a later period – the period dominated by fiction – the view of the novel as an escape from real life was blurred by the fact that, for example, Dickens was saying something which was urgently relative to real-life problems. Best-selling fiction of the early twentieth century had to take account of the fact that most of the potential readers were in greater or lesser degree looking for a kind of escape, the word being used in no censorious sense. Reading, like golf and bridge, had to play its part in pro-viding the material for 'really living' for a man or a woman in these blessed reaches of the week when he or she was free from the tasks, whatever their nature, which were performed less out of enjoyment for work than because the performance of those tasks was the only way to 'keep things going'.

A common faith, a common cause, a common objective help greatly the 'alleviation' spoken of by T. H. Green. Faith in Christianity (not quite the same thing as Christian faith but socially cohesive) was still powerful in 1900; but in this connec-tion the important point is that its power was visibly diminishing and had been diminishing for half a century. It is here the sense of change, the element of uncertainty which counts. The Empire had provided a large number of people, particularly in the middle-class Mandarinate, with a similar sense of common cause and common objective. It is pointless to draw attention in this context to the gulf between what such people supposed the Em-pire to be and what it really was. The essential is that they had seen it as the indispensable protector and purveyor of civilization; a worthy cause directed to worthy objectives.

But, to take a single instance, the Boer War – or rather the widespread opposition to it in Britain – had subjected this creed to a questioning, an investigation, more rigorous than it had suffered before except in relatively restricted circles of society. It was questioned on moral grounds. More importantly perhaps it began to be questioned by some of those who a few years earlier had been among the most enthusiastic inflators of the imperial idea. Kipling's admonition to 'take up the White Man's burden' has often been misunderstood. Many people even today assume that the old imperialist bard was addressing the younger generation of English people, urging them to further efforts in the colonialization of India, Africa, and other possibly available areas. On the contrary, the poem, published in *McClure's Magazine* for 1 February 1899, was addressed not to the British but to the Americans, then in a state of moral crisis over the surge of American imperialism in the Philippines. Properly read it implied that the capacity of the British to sustain the imperial burden had been strained to its limit. It was for the Americans to carry on where the British had stopped. The poem's pessimism on that score is of a piece with the mood of *Recessional*, with its references – most untimely and uncalled-for, as less thoughtful imperialists felt – to the 'pomp of yesterday' and the fate of Nineveh and Tyre. People looking nearer home for signs of change and possible decay could observe preparations for the electrification of the London Underground Railway and the construction of the first Tube. These undertakings were to be financed in the main by Americans.

As for what we may call the 'creed of the common objective' it will be pointed out that in a class-divided society no such objective has existed or can exist except in times of war or other major national emergency. But if we are thinking not of the nation as a whole but of one section of it, namely the middle class, then the literary evidence seems to show that the middle class towards and after the turn of the century was becoming increasingly divided on the question of desirable objectives. As Lady Frances Balfour wrote of the period, 'Ill winds were blowing hard through society.' To take a blatant example: Mrs Pankhurst organized the militant suffragettes in 1903. It is true that the majority of the middle class regarded this development with emotion escalating from derision to fear and horror. It is, on the other hand, equally true that there was never a majority of the middle class standing in enthusiastic support of the brutal methods used against the suffragettes by the police and the government. A considerable sector of the middle class, while 'deploring' the methods of the militants, more or less passionately believed that the way to eliminate such methods was to make serious concessions to the suffragettes.

These divisions were apparent at the very surface of political and social life. But they, like the suffragette movement itself, were expressions of divisions at a deeper level. The suffragette movement did not appear suddenly out of nowhere. It was the outward and visible sign in 1903 of profound uncertainties.

In view of all this, it is no longer surprising that the middle-class reader should have been drawn to – should even have demanded – a long look at people and situations activated by some kind of just intelligible religious fanaticism. And that phenomenon can be observed, reflecting the doubts and divisions of the middle class, in British literature throughout the first half of the twentieth century.

The deep blue yonder

THE PACIFIC OCEAN with its many small islands has appealed to the European imagination even more strongly than the Sahara Desert with its oases. The appeal has differed widely from generation to generation, and, in so doing, has thrown flickering light on the state of that imagination. Robinson Crusoe's island was no tourist attraction. For the mass of readers it was the convenient setting for an enthralling adventure-story centring on one man's experiments in survival. To others it was, as Defoe intended, a contribution to thought about man as a strictly economic animal and in terms of man as an individual divorced from any political or social community. People were passionately interested alike in the adventures of Robinson Crusoe and in their social implications. Few wished to go to a desert island themselves. They believed, as Professor Ian Watt points out in *The Rise of the Novel*, that 'Just as society has made every individual what he is, the prolonged lack of society actually tends to make the individual relapse into a straitened primitivism of thought and feeling. In Defoe's sources for *Robinson Crusoe* what actually happened to the castaways was at best uninspiring. At worst, harassed by fear and dogged by ecological degradation, they sank more and more to the level of animals, lost the use of speech, went mad, or died of inanition. One book which Defoe had almost certainly read, *The Voyages and Travels of J. Albert de Mandelslo,* tells of two such cases: of a Frenchman who after two years of solitude on Mauritius, tore his clothing to pieces in a fit of madness brought on by a diet of raw tortoise; and of a Dutch seaman on St Helena who disinterred the body of a buried comrade, and set out to sea in the coffin.'

These realities of absolute solitude were in keeping with the traditional view of its effects as expressed by Dr Johnson; the 'solitary mortal', he averred, was 'certainly luxurious, probably superstitious, and possibly mad; the mind stagnates for want of employment; grows morbid, and is extinguished like a candle in foul air.'

In a fine analytical passage Professor Watt goes on to point out that for all his knowledge of what really happens on desert islands, Defoe played a trick on his readers in their urban and village communities. He 'departs from psychological probability in order to redeem his picture of man's inexorable solitariness and it is for this reason that he appeals very strongly to all who feel isolated – and who at times does not? An inner voice continually suggests to us that the human isolation which individualism has fostered is painful and tends ultimately to a life of apathetic animality and mental derangement; Defoe answers confidently that it can be made the arduous prelude to the fuller realization of every individual's potentialities; and the solitary readers of two centuries of individualism cannot but applaud so convincing an example of making a virtue out of a necessity, so cheering a colouring to that universal image of individualist experience, solitude.'

Thus to solitary urban man or woman the fictional survival and triumph of the typically solitary Robinson Crusoe provides a spiritual tonic.

In novels of much later periods the theme appears in cruder form. The fictional picture of people who have got away from it all acts sometimes as a tonic, sometimes as a sedative. It is a vision of a physical world where the goads, nuisances, harassments, and sheer noise, physical and mental, which beset urban man are eliminated. There is an agreeable emphasis on the physical. When it comes to spearing the fish and climbing coconut trees, not to mention fighting off hostile islanders, the physically fit man will have a better chance to display his qualities even than on the golf course or tennis court. Sometimes the fact of getting away from it all is performed not by imaginary geographical movement, but by movement in time. Nostalgia for an imaginary past plays a large role in the conversation of characters in popular bestsellers, and in the comments and asides permitted themselves by the authors. Some time, somewhere, they insist, there must have been a simpler, purer life than we know. There must have been a life with less hurry and bustle in it; a life of relative leisure; a life without a rat-race. The illusion of a happy land long, long ago is as soothing, perhaps even stimulating, to the reader as the illusion of that same happy land far, far away. It is the purely fantasy form of another common activity – that is, the writing of history backwards, so that the past, or some section of the past, appears to confirm or justify some political attitude of the present time.

It has of course been remarked that those who take pleasure in imagining themselves existing in some earlier period of history almost invariably assume that this retrograde reincarnation will find them occupying some position reasonably high on the social and financial ladder. They may not be born again as lords, but at least they will not be toiling peasants or small farmers threatened with ruin by eviction, or, still less, inmates of a debtors' prison. In whatever sphere it operates Walter Mittyism tends to elevate.

The Blue Lagoon by H. de Vere Stacpoole almost perfectly exemplifies what readers wanted, and for that matter still want, from the Pacific Island novel. (The Malayan novel and the roughly Indonesian novel are of course a different pair of shoes.) Published in January 1908, it ran into sixteen editions before the assassination at Sarajevo in 1914. Had a computer been available to de Vere Stacpoole and his publisher Fisher Unwin, they could not have done better than they did. All the appeals are there. It is no wonder that so many people who may have pretended to be tackling Bennett were in fact swimming in the Blue Lagoon.

The basic message, simply illuminating an attitude, is spelled out in the last chapter. A rich man, in search of his son and niece, who disappeared in the Pacific years ago, is discussing savages with the captain of the search-vessel.

> ' "Look here," said the captain, "it's all very well talking, but upon my word I think that we civilized folk put on a lot of airs and waste a lot of pity on savages."
>
> "How so?"
>
> "What does a man want to be but happy?"
>
> "Yes."
>
> "Well, who is happier than a naked savage in a warm climate? Oh, he is happy enough and he is not always holding a corroboree. He's a good deal of a gentleman; he has

perfect health, he lives the life a man was born to live face to face with Nature, he doesn't see the sun from his window, or the moon through the smoke of a factory chimney; happy and civilized too – but bless you, where is he? the whites have driven him out."

"Suppose . . ." said Lestrange [he is the man looking for his son and niece cast away in the Pacific], "Suppose those children had been brought up face to face with Nature – "

"Yes?"

"Living that free life – "

"Yes?"

"Waking up under the stars" – Lestrange was speaking with his eyes fixed as if upon something far away – "going to sleep as the sun sets, feeling the air fresh like this which blows upon us all around them, suppose they were like that, would it not be a cruelty to bring them back to what we call civilization?"

"I think it would," said Stannistreet.'

Thoughtful brooding at about this level is offered lavishly throughout the book. To ask whether the talented author took this sort of philosophizing seriously is irrelevant for anyone looking at the book as a window through which to observe the readers. De Vere Stacpoole was a masterly artificer. He was a cook who knew the correct ingredients of a palatable stew; a doctor who knew just what to order for the nervous patient who looked abroad and saw the Germans building Dreadnoughts; looked at home and saw Tom Mann, Ernest Bevin, and Victor Grayson raging subversively through docks, workshops, and slums; looked across the sea to Ireland and saw more guns than leprechauns; looked out of those office windows and saw the undersized and poorly nourished masses hurrying back and forth; looked at the social and domestic life of himself and his friends and at least surmised it might be threatened by novel and disruptive ideas, possibly by disruptive and over-permissive actions.

To live a free life face to face with Nature and be 'a good deal of a gentleman' at the same time – that made a fine dream for the man on his way home from a strenuous city gamble in Kaffirs. He could go to the theatre. There he was liable to see Galsworthy's *Strife* raising nerve-racking problems of industrial conflict, or, if he could still get tickets for it, du Maurier's *An Englishman's House*. That was the one where England is credibly and terrifyingly invaded by the armies of the 'Emperor of the North'.

After such experiences how agreeable to go to bed with the seventh edition of *The Blue Lagoon*. One has only to glance through the contents pages to feel confident that this is going to be a worth-while charter flight away from it all. Romance, adventure and much besides are yours even before take-off. The chapter-headings beckon:

> '*Under the Stars. Dawn on a Wide Wide Sea. Shadows in the Moonlight. The Tragedy of the Boats. The Lake of Azure. Death Veiled with Lichen. Fair Pictures in the Blue. The Poetry of Learning. The Devil's Cask. The Dreamer on the Reef. The Garland of Flowers. Alone. Half Child – Half Savage. The Demon of the Reef. What Beauty Concealed. The Sound of a Drum. Love Steps in. The Sleep of Paradise. An Island Honeymoon. The Vanishing of Emmeline. The Vanishing of Emmeline* (continued). *The Newcomer. The Lagoon of Fire. A Fallen Idol. The Stricken Woods. The Hand of the Sea. Together.*'

There was nothing false about that prospectus. The basic scenario was old and reliable – Crusoe-and-soda, all the romance of Defoe with only ten per cent of the realism. Incidental ingredients included a truly realistic and eerie depiction of escape from a burning ship, with the survivors in the boats murdering one another for water; a battle with an octopus; incursion of bloodthirsty kanaka and ruffianly white whalers; a hair-raising cyclone; a lurking death-dealing shark.

Also on display was a larger-than-life-size Irish seaman with a fiddle under his ear, and songs, ballads and magic legends constantly on his lips in the correct Celtic manner. With rare skill, Stacpoole succeeded in presenting a satisfying picture in full colour of an Englishman's idea of an Irishman, and at the same time enlivening this stagey figure with some trappings of harsh reality. He dies uglily, dead drunk on the coral reef of the island. The two children whom he has rescued from the burning ship, thinking him asleep, creep up to play a little

game with him. Then a crab runs out of his dead mouth, and
half of his face is seen to have been eaten away by larvae.

But these enthralling episodes are not allowed to obscure – at
least not for long – the main theme, developed with slowly
tautening tension and maximum suspense.

From the moment that the eight-year-old boy and girl cousins
set foot beneath 'the cocoa palms and breadfruit trees, inter-
mixed with the mammee apple and the tendrils of the wild vine',
every attentive reader of the chapter-headings realized that, if
all the advertised excitements, beauty spots and significant
spots were to be duly visited, they were likely to be resident
on that island for quite a while. It was an island upon which
all was 'sharply outlined – burning, coloured, arrogant yet ten-
der – heartbreakingly beautiful, for the spirit of eternal morning
was here, eternal happiness, eternal youth.' And what the eager
reader could hardly wait to find out was just what on earth
was going to happen when those two kids reached the age of
puberty?

Readers had to wait for the answer until page 181. But it
was not a dull time of waiting. There was no need to skip. For
many pages before that, the growing boy and girl displayed
themselves in a slow, essentially pure Edwardian strip-tease,
partially or wholly naked, and getting handsomer in body month
by month.

'They crossed over to the reef, where as usual Dick divested
himself of his clothing. It was strange that out here he would
go about stark naked, yet on the island he always wore some
covering. But not so strange, perhaps, after all.

The sea is a great purifier, both of the mind and the body;
before that great, sweet spirit people do not think in the same
way as they think far inland. What woman would appear
in a town, or on a country road, or even bathing in a river,
as she appears bathing in the sea?'

For several pages both of them have been feeling a little
unusual; not exactly off-colour, but edgy. Now they sit down to
rest and eat fruit at the feet of a five-thousand-year-old stone
idol, thirty feet high, with an aura of mystery and fear. The
girl Emmeline is bending a cane into the form of a bow when

'it slipped, flew out and struck her companion a sharp blow on the side of his face. Almost on the instant he turned and slapped her on the shoulder. She stared at him for a moment in troubled amazement, a sob came in her throat.

Then some veil seemed lifted, some wizard's wand stretched out, some mysterious vial broken. As she looked at him like that, he suddenly and fiercely clasped her in his arms. He held her like this for a moment, dazed, stupefied, not knowing what to do. Then her lips told him, for they met his in an endless kiss.'

Comes the moon, and

'peeping over the trees, she looked down into the valley, where the great idol of stone had kept its solitary vigil for five thousand years, perhaps, or more. At his base, in his shadow, looking as if under his protection, lay two human beings, naked, clasped in each other's arms, and fast asleep. One could scarcely pity his vigil had it been marked some-times through the years by such an incident as this. The thing had been conducted just as the birds conduct their love affairs. An affair absolutely natural, absolutely blameless and without sin. It was a marriage according to nature, without feast or guests, consummated with accidental cynicism under the shadow of a religion a thousand years dead.

So happy in their ignorance were they, that they only knew that suddenly life had changed, that the skies and seas were bluer, and that they had become in some magical way one a part of the other. The birds on the tree above were equally as happy in their ignorance and in their love.'

The publishers described the book as 'powerful', an adjective which at the time seems to have had faintly X-certificate con-notations. But *Punch* was able to justify its high recommenda-tion of the book by pointing out that it was 'healthily nurtured on the fruits of an observation which knows when not to observe'. To Edwardian intellectuals such an assurance might have appeared rather as a slur than a recommendation. But it gave confidence to the library public of 1908 – 1914. Not many years before, that public in Britain might have preferred to have its attention more firmly directed to the birds, whose loves could have delicately symbolized the human situation on the ground. Not many years later, they did not require the natural activity and bliss of the birds to be trotted out as justification for human goings-on. Stacpoole usefully indicates just where the Edwardian public drew the line. (It is not entirely clear whether the copulation of Dick and Emmeline would have been so acceptable had it not taken place so very close to the 'great, sweet spirit' of the purifying sea.)

We soon learn the reason for 'the vanishing of Emmeline' twice mentioned in the chapter-headings. She has gone into the woods to have a baby boy. A most cute little fellow. Grows hair, cuts a tooth, excites paternal and maternal love just like a baby in a pram outside Harrods. Shows signs of intelligence, too. 'Ah me! we laugh at young mothers, and all the miraculous things they tell us about their babies. They see what we cannot see; the first unfolding of that mysterious flower, the mind.'

The question, so important to public and publisher, is : Will the ending be happy or unhappy? With his unerring sense of the taste of his period, Stacpoole arranges that it shall be susceptible of being regarded as both at the same time. Naked tragedy would be going a bit far, and be unsuitably reminiscent of real life. On the other hand, anything too jolly could appear vulgar, and lacking in that resonance of the deeper note which was indispensable if one were to read, without some sense of guilt, this type of novel in serious times like these.

By a series of mishaps, Dick, Emmeline and the baby find themselves being swept in their tiny dinghy out of the lagoon into the limitless ocean. The sculls have been lost overboard. Their pet bird has flown back in panic to the land. All they have left in the boat is a bunch of crimson berries Emmeline had earlier, accidentally, snapped from a tree. These are 'the never-wake-up berries. The berries that will cause a man to sleep, should he eat of them – to sleep and dream, and never wake up again.'

Adrift on the ocean without hope of material rescue, they are rescued, in another sense, by the berries.

'All the wonders in their short existence had culminated in this final wonder, this passing away together from the world of Time. This strange voyage they had embarked on – to where? . . . They were together. Come what might, nothing

could divide them; even should they sleep and never wake
up, they would sleep together . . . Clasped in Emmeline's hand
was the last and most mysterious gift of the mysterious world
they had known – the branch of crimson berries.'

Harsh critics could claim that the crimson berry sequence
was no less than an incitement to the making of suicide pacts.
Others more percipient might find in the steamy philosophy of
The Blue Lagoon a genteel, middle-class reflection of the fierce
political revolutionary anarchism which at the turn of the century exploded in so many bombings and assassinations; in what
was called by the anarchists 'the propaganda of the deed' against
the State, and against the whole fabric of society.

Naturally to be accused of 'anarchism', even of in any sense
'reflecting' it, would have seemed both horrifying and absurdly
paradoxical to most members of the British library public. Yet
what do we find them reading? They dream that the man
outside society and civilization – the savage – is happier and
better than the man running in the society rat-race. Modern
society is a prison for the spirit of man. Try to blow it up with
bombs, or get away from it all on a dream-boat to the Mar-
quesas. To mate like the birds is lovelier than conventional
marriage with 'feast and guests'. And for the dreamer it is possible to accept this while being prepared to denounce, as part
of a subversionary plot against Church and State, the supposed
views of the anarchists on the subject of 'free love'.

Since the dream-life by that Bluest of Lagoons cannot be
transferred to Knightsbridge without thus disrupting Harrods
and all that that implies, Stacpoole's disposal of the lovers and
their baby is the ideal solution. The spirit of it was echoed a
long time later in a song popular in the United States and
Britain after the Wall Street crash of 1929 :

> '*No more money in the bank,*
> *No cute baby we can spank,*
> *What's to do about it?*
> *Let's put out the light*
> *And go to sleep.*'

The message, or philosophy if it can be so termed, of *The*

Blue Lagoon, however hazy and insubstantial, was certainly not of a nature to please that increasing number of more or less vocal British people who thought that what the country needed was to be roughly awakened to the German menace, and not only to be awake and aware of it, as so many people already were, but to take muscle-flexing action to meet it.

Into battle

THE FIRST EXPLOSIVE charge successfully detonated in the sporadic Cold War which preceded the war of 1914 was loosed off in 1903 by a man of thirty, fresh from fighting the Boers, and until then quite unknown to the general public.

At that date British opinion about Germany was incoherent. There were those – there always are – who living a little behind the times found it impossible to regard as a serious potential enemy any nation other than France. Even the Kaiser's encouraging telegram to President Kruger after the Boers' repulse of the Jameson Raid, though it had jolted their estimates of possible friend and foe, had not destroyed their traditional position. Others, while recognizing with regret that possibly the Kaiser and certainly the German Admiralty and the German armament barons could be considered a menace, thought that the mass of the German people, and particularly the German mercantile middle class, were possibly friendly and certainly pacific. That class of German, it was supposed, was as inclined as its opposite number in Britain to accept the view that, under conditions of modern industrial capitalism, financiers, industrialists, and merchants of all kinds in all countries must realize that war could only be inimical, and perhaps fatal, to their interests. The pressure of their opinion would curb alike the extravagances of the Kaiser and the sinister ambitions of the Admirals. Such opinions ran parallel to those of the socialists and radicals in both countries who had a similar faith in the desire, the will, and the ability of the working class to exert itself internationally to foil and overthrow war-makers everywhere.

In 1903 those who saw the rise of German economic, military, and naval power as the chief threat, increasing year by year, to the power and even the independence of Britain were not loudly heard from. Yet when Erskine Childers, the young

Anglo-Irishman, published *The Riddle of the Sands*, of which the
central theme was a dramatic, even melodramatic, warning to
Britain regarding German aims and British vulnerability, its success was so large and so immediate that it seemed to prove the
existence in at least the subconscious of great numbers of English
people of a feeling about Germany not shared by any of the
groups just mentioned. It could be argued that *The Riddle of the
Sands* was a finely written adventure story and furthermore a
story of adventure at sea, supposed at least to have a particular
appeal to English readers. Another ingredient, useful in achieving
popular success, was the fact that the adventurous enterprise
was undertaken by two quite normal British middle-class Oxford
graduates, took place in sea areas quite close to Britain, and
was performed in a small boat of the kind which many even
moderately well-to-do middle-class Englishmen might own, or
hope to own. But it is next to impossible to believe that these
qualities by themselves would have given the book the impetus
and impact which it had. In this connection the Foreword to
the 1931 edition written by M. A. Childers is both significant
and somewhat melancholy. It states:

'In *The Riddle of the Sands*, first published in 1903, Erskine
Childers advocated preparedness for war as being the best
preventive of war. During the years that followed, he funda-
mentally altered his opinion. His profound study of military
history, of politics, and later of the causes of the Great War
convinced him that preparedness induced war. It was not
only that to the vast numbers of people engaged in the fostered
war services and armament industries, war meant the exercise
of their professions and trades and the advancement of their
interests; preparedness also led to international armament
rivalries, and bred in the minds of the nations concerned
fears, antagonisms, and ambitions, that were destructive to
peace.

Whatever the views held by readers upon this question, the
book remains the cherished companion of those who love the
sea and who put forth in great or small sailing ships in search
of adventure and magical contentment to be won by strenuous
endeavour.

To such ardent adventurers and to the younger generation
who hope to follow them, this book is offered anew by a little

company of sea lovers who hold it in trust for the known and
unknown friends of Erskine Childers.'

It is, as I say, melancholy to see a writer having the utmost
goodwill towards Childers seeking in the last two paragraphs
of this foreword to 'de-politicalize' his book and reduce it to
the status of a stimulus for Sea Scouts. To de-politicalize Childers
is like trying to take the incendiary matter out of an incendiary
bomb. As a political activist Childers was unique among the bestsellers of his time. No 'adventure story' of our age could surpass
in quality the tragic adventure of Erskine Childers' real life.
By 1914 the man who had done so much to rouse the British
middle class to prepare for war was steering his own yacht
Asgard into Howth Harbour, Dublin, with 900 rifles and 29,000
rounds of ammunition for the Volunteer Army of Ireland
dedicated to resist both the Orangemen of the north and if necessary the British Government in the defence of Irish freedom.
It was a cause to which Childers thereafter dedicated his life
and his extraordinary abilities. For any cause in which he believed, he was a propagandist of genius. By hindsight it can
be observed that this quality was already evident in the manufacture of a 'suspense novel' dealing with adventure at sea,
and a vehicle for the message of *The Riddle of the Sands*. In
1921 he was appointed to the strenuous and, in every political
and physical sense, perilous job of Director of Publicity for the
Irish Republicans. In the same year he was Secretary to the
Irish delegation which negotiated in Dublin the treaty with
Lloyd George. When he saw what kind of treaty was going to
emerge from those negotiations, Childers urged the delegates
not to sign, and later denounced the treaty in the Dail. When
acceptance of the treaty brought civil war to Ireland, Childers,
passionately convinced that the treaty left Ireland still virtually
under the domination of British imperialists, joined de Valera
and the Republicans in their battles against the Government of
the new Free State. At the height of the civil war Childers
continued to run his potent printing press from a deserted barracks near Macroom and later from a two-roomed cottage in
the hills. Kevin O'Higgins, Minister for Home Affairs in the
Free State Government, in supporting a resolution calling for
emergency powers for the army, directed his attack chiefly
against Childers, saying :

'I know that the able Englishman who is leading those who
are opposed to this Government has his eyes quite definitely
on one objective, and that is the complete breakdown of the
economic and social fabric so that this thing that is trying so
hard to be an Irish nation will go down in chaos, anarchy
and futility. His programme is a negative programme, a purely
destructive programme, and it would be victory to him and his
peculiar mind if he prevents the Government coming into
existence under the terms of the treaty signed in London last
December. He has no constructive programme, and so he
keeps steadily, callously and ghoulishly at his career of striking at the heart of this nation, striking deadly, or what he
hopes are deadly, blows at the economic life of this nation.'

It was a tribute to the effectiveness and in particular to the
power of words (for Childers held no high military position)
which has been claimed for very few writers. He was captured
at last. By a gruesome paradox, Winston Churchill, who had
benefited so much from the 'preparedness' propaganda in Britain
before the outbreak of the First World War, greeted the news
in a speech at Dundee with the vindictive words: 'I have seen
with satisfaction that the mischief-making murderous renegade,
Erskine Childers, has been captured. No man has done more
harm or shown more genuine malice, or endeavoured to bring a
greater curse on the common people of Ireland than this strange
being, actuated by a deadly and malignant hatred for the land
of his birth. Such as he is may all who hate us be.'

After a secret trial and while his appeal was still pending,
Childers was hurriedly shot by the military authorities of the
Free State at Beggars Bush Barracks on 24 November 1922.

In Ireland he is reverenced as the hero who died in the cause
of liberation. The English look upon him as the author of a
long-term best-seller, of which the original purpose has been
almost forgotten, a book which is only remembered and re-read
as a sound story about amateur sailors facing dangers at sea
off the German North Sea coast.

An exciting yarn it certainly is. The narrator is a young man
of fashion, doing well alike at the Foreign Office and in Society.
The accident of some shifts of plan and personnel in the highest
quarters had resulted in his being forced to postpone his summer
leave and remain in London in August and September. Cut

off from house parties, shooting parties, yachting parties, and the society of lovely débutantes, he sinks into desperate boredom and a sense of martyrdom. As a gambit for a novel his situation is not unlike that of Richard Hannay at the beginning of *The Thirty-Nine Steps*. Hannay, too, is desperately bored with London and ready to welcome any event which may relieve the tedium. In his case the event takes the form of the arrival, and subsequent murder by an agent of the Black Stone, of the paranoid secret agent Scudder. For Carruthers, narrator of *The Riddle of the Sands*, the event is the arrival of a letter from a man he has known moderately well at Oxford inviting him to go cruising with him in the Baltic. Eating dinner in a strange club, his own being closed, he reviews the pros and cons of accepting the invitation which has been sent from the yacht *Dulcibella* at Flensburg in Schleswig Holstein. 'When I reached the savoury I had concluded, so far as I had centred my mind on it at all, that the whole thing was a culminating irony, as, indeed, was the savoury in its way. After the wreck of my pleasant plans and the fiasco of my martyrdom, to be asked as consolation to spend October freezing in the Baltic with an eccentric nonentity who bored me was ironic.'

Of course he changes his mind and accepts. He nearly changes it again on finding that the *Dulcibella* is small, rugged, and uncomfortable, and that his friend, a passionate sailor, is dedicated to yachting the hard way. The elegant Carruthers, who previously when he thought of yachting thought of Cowes, is appalled. At the outset there is a good deal of friction between himself and his future companion, Davies. But Carruthers soon learns to admire certain qualities of Davies and things appear to be about to proceed smoothly. Carruthers, however, is mystified by certain entries, and still more by certain omissions, in the log of the *Dulcibella* kept by Davies on his outward voyage eastward among the Frisian Islands off the north-west German coast. Soon, too, he is considerably shaken by the realization that Davies' invitation to cruise with him to the Baltic was a deception : Davies, for reasons not immediately disclosed, is in fact determined to get back to the Frisians and the channels among the sands between those islands and the mainland coast of Germany.

Davies explains the history of the log. On his outward voyage he made the acquaintance of the owner of a big yacht, a Herr

Dollman, and of his beautiful daughter. On the pretext of showing Davies a short cut to their destination, Dollman made an attempt to lure him and the *Dulcibella* to destruction.

At the end of his enthralling narrative, Davies suddenly discloses to Carruthers that it was the encounter with Dollman and the conclusions which he drew from it that prompted him to write his letter inviting Carruthers to join him. 'You see,' says Davies, 'I have come to the conclusion that that chap was a spy.'

'In the end it came out quite quietly and suddenly, and left me in profound amazement. "I wired to you—that chap was a spy." It was the close association of these two ideas that hit me hardest at the moment. For a second I was back in the dreary splendour of the London club rooms, spelling out that crabbed scrawl from Davies and fastidiously criticizing his proposal in the light of a holiday. Holiday! What was to be its issue? Chilling and opaque as the fog that filtered through the skylight, there flooded my imagination a mist of doubt and fear. "A spy!" I repeated blankly. "What do you mean? Why did you write to me? A spy of what – of whom?"

"I'll tell you how I worked it out," said Davies. "I don't think spy is the right word; but I mean something pretty bad." '

Davies is already determined to find out just what evil work Dollman is engaged on with regard to the West in the sands of the Frisian Islands. Carruthers is gradually brought to share his enthusiasm. Together they sail back through the Kiel Canal into the North Sea. After adventures which would be exciting enough, certainly to anyone interested or capable of being stirred by 'sea stories', even without the mystery of Dollman and whatever lies behind it, they ultimately hit upon the truth. It is that the sands and their channels are being used to prepare a secret base from which will be launched a lightning seaborne invasion of England. The Kaiser himself is personally interested in this grandiose plan which is depicted as the very centre of German political and naval strategy. He comes down, incognito, but recognized by Carruthers, to view a rehearsal of the invasion.

Erskine Childers' preface to the book is particularly interesting. In it he asserts that he really had a friend whom he has called 'Carruthers', and that the book itself is a faithful recital of Carruthers' narrative. It is not clear whether this is really the case or whether, as is more probable, the preface is simply intended to give an extra verisimilitude to the body of the book. The question is relatively unimportant. What is important about the preface is that in it Childers expresses with vigour his critical attitude towards the British defence authorities.

'At the end of the narrative – which, from its bearing on studies and speculations of my own, as well as from its intrinsic interest and racy delivery, made a very deep impression on me – Carruthers added that the important fact discovered in the course of the trip had without a moment's delay been communicated to the proper authorities, who, after some dignified incredulity, due in part, perhaps, to the pitiful inadequacy of their own Secret Service, had, he believed, made use of them to avert a great national danger. I say "he believed" for although it was beyond question that the danger was averted for the time, it was doubtful whether they had stirred a foot to combat it, the secret discovered being of such a nature that mere suspicion of it on this side was likely to destroy its efficacy.

But political tendencies were driving them to reconsider their decision. These showed with disastrous plainness that the information wrung with such peril and labour from the German Government and transmitted so promptly to our own had had none but the most transitory effect, if any, on our policy. On the contrary, some poisonous influence, whose origin still baffled all but a very few, was persistently at work to drive back our diplomacy into paths which even without this clarion warning they would be wise on principle to shun. As a drastic cure for what had come to be nothing less than a national disease, the two friends now had a mind to make their story public; and it was about this that "Carruthers" wished for my advice. The great drawback was that an Englishman, bearing an honoured name, was disgracefully implicated, and that unless infinite delicacy were used, innocent persons, and, especially, a young lady, would suffer pain and indignity, if his identity was known. Indeed troublesome rumours, containing a grain of truth and a mass of falsehood, were already afloat.'

If the preface was in fact simply there to impress the reader with the actuality and reality of the story, it is a good early example of Erskine Childers' skill as a propagandist.

Between publication of *The Riddle of the Sands* and 1914, the number of books designed either to rouse the British public to the reality of the German menace or to take advantage of the growing 'scare' proliferated. They were on various levels, none of them approaching that of *The Riddle of the Sands.* William Le Queux wrote a novel on the subject which was serialized in Northcliffe's *Daily Mail.*

And yet it is a fact that to expect something to happen, and to have expected it for some time, in no way reduces one's surprise when it actually does happen. For Western man, the First World War was a series of surprise-packages, each more startlingly horrible than the last. That was so despite the warnings which had been uttered for years. The people who declared they had 'seen it coming' were right, but that was all they were right about. They had in no way indicated what it would really be like. It was as though Jehovah had noticed that humans were trying to outguess Him, and decided to show them just how humiliatingly little they knew of the tricks He had up His sleeve. Because the outbreak of international war had been so generally expected and because by hindsight it looks as though everything that did happen had to happen, the shock effect of the sheer surprisingness of things as they really occurred can be much underestimated, or even imagined with difficulty. It was astonishment, as well as horror and dismay, which shook the Western mind more severely than it had been shaken at any time since the French Revolution.

After the War was over, everyone sneered at those who in August 1914 had constantly stated that the whole thing would be ended by Christmas. The Kaiser had told his troops, 'When the leaves fall you will have peace.' What fools, one thinks. And then recalls that in 1939 the British Imperial Defence Committee officially reported to the Government that within two months of the outbreak of the Second World War bombs would have killed 400,000 Londoners and wounded three quarters of a million more, leaving the city an uninhabitable ruin.

In 1939, as in 1914, it was generally though not universally assumed that the destructive power of modern weapons, terrible as it was, would at least ensure a short war. In both cases the predictors had a surprise coming.

Obviously all history is a form of hindsight. Historians do their best to correct this faulty vision by study of contemporary documents. Among these, particularly in a period when print was still the chief means of mass communication, bestsellers probably rate higher in terms of the light they shed on what people thought and why, than official archives and even the diaries of individuals.

One of the great bestsellers of 1915, Ian Hay's *The First Hundred Thousand*, is a case in point. For, by the fact of being a bestseller, a book of this kind, a semi-fictionalized reportage, is seen to be disclosing both what people wanted to believe and also what they could accept as credible. And hindsight can do the rest.

The established literary men of 1914 were quick off the mark. The public expected it of them. As the corporal yelled to the inarticulate officer half a minute before the platoon was going to march over the edge of the cliff, 'For Gawd's sake say something, even if it's only goodbye.' Arnold Bennett said something. Wells said something. Hilaire Belloc launched a magazine called *Land and Sea* which explained war fortnightly. John Buchan almost immediately began a history of the conflict.

Captain John H. Beith, 'Ian Hay', was a relatively minor figure, known as the author of *Pip* and *A Man's Man*. At the outbreak of war he joined the Argyll and Sutherland Highlanders, fought gallantly, and got the M.C. But in relation to the total war effort, his major contribution was *The First Hundred Thousand*, a running account, issued monthly in *Blackwood's Magazine* and as a book in 1915, of 'K1' – Kitchener's First Army – written from the inside.

The book had two objectives, both achieved. One was simply to give an authentic picture of a way of life which was as novel and surprising to most British people as that of hitherto unknown tribes in Central Africa. The other was, so to say, to 'sell' this way of life to the public: to strengthen and enliven the public morale by showing how, despite 'unpreparedness', lack of equipment, and ghastly top-level blunderings, common knowledge of which tended to create alarm and despondency, the indomitable spirit of the race would overcome some day, probably some day fairly soon.

To a much later generation, accustomed to see 1914 as the red dawn of a long doomsday, the ebullient, sometimes acerbic, gaiety of the book can appear almost shocking. Nor was it a phoney gaiety assumed for propaganda purposes. At least it seems to me that nobody reading the book without too much hindsight could doubt that ebullient gaiety was a genuine part of the scene. (One may recall the atmosphere in Madrid in 1936 when the first Republican militia battalions were being formed to do battle with Franco.)

Equally surprising is the savagely satirical treatment of High Command, meaning in particular the War Office and the Treasury. It is curious to reflect how little of this criticism would, in the supposedly more democratic days of 1939, have passed the censor. This may in part be attributed to the relative inefficiency and unsophistication of the censorship in 1914, but there is more to it than that. For it is apparent that in 1914 the authorities, besides being incompetent, were a great deal less nervously mistrustful of public opinion than they were in 1939. If the politico-military censorship was ramshackle that was partly due to inexperience, but partly, also, to the conscious or subconscious assumption that in a 'free country' it could scarcely be anything else. That was a time when to most people the word 'security' simply meant being safe. By 1939, under fearful pressures, it had come to mean a reason – good, bad, or just lazy – for tying a muzzle on any dog watchful or malign enough to bark.

Looked at from another angle, the change of attitude indicated an awareness of the growth of literacy. To this extent there was no paradox in the fact of a more democratic society being subjected to a more rigorous censorship than seemed necessary in 1914. The impact of the printed word could be more extensive and thus potentially more dangerous.

Ian Hay, lumping War Office, Treasury, and the Army Ordnance Office together under the general title 'Olympus', further subdivides Olympus into the Round Game Department, the Fairy Godmother Department, and the Practical Joke Department. He lists, in detail, the more or less deleterious activities of these Departments, with the clear implication that the highest authorities are either moronic or malignant.

Thus, if the Practical Joke Department can manoeuvre its

'helpless pawns into Mudsplosh Camp' it scores 'ten whole points' in the game.

'We are in Mudsplosh Camp today. In transferring us here the Department secured full points, including bonus. Let it not be supposed, however, that we are decrying our present quarters. Mudsplosh Camp is – or is going to be – a notably planned and admirably equipped military centre. At present it consists of some three hundred wooden huts, in all stages of construction, covering about twenty acres of high moorland. The huts are heated with stoves, and will be delightfully warm when we get some coal. They are lit by – or rather wired for – electric light. Meanwhile a candle-end does well enough for a room only a hundred feet long. There are numerous other adjuncts to our comfort – wash-houses, for instance. These will be invaluable, when the water is laid on . . . There is a spacious dining-hall and as soon as the roof is on, our successors or their successors will make merry therein. Meanwhile, there are worse places to eat one's dinner than the floor – the mud outside, for instance. The stables are lofty and well ventilated. Pending their completion, the horses and mules are very comfortable, picketed on the edge of the moor. After all, there are only sixty of them, and most of them have rugs; and it can't possibly go on snowing for ever.'

An officer serving with his battalion in the Second World War who tried to get away with that sort of thing would have found himself in very hot water. And any magazine that published it would have faced at least threats of suppression. In general, the whole tone could be denounced as apt to undermine public confidence in the Army Command, while at the same time giving aid and comfort to the enemy. Furthermore the passage is a flagrant breach of 'security'. From it the enemy can, for instance, estimate the exact state of construction reached in a major British Army camp. Such information, from an obviously inside source, pieced together with other bits of information can be an invaluable record of military developments in Britain. Be it noted that the writer slips into his account the *exact number* of horses and mules attached to the unit in question. A professional spy could not have done better.

The strictly contemporary quality, resulting, in part, from the monthly publication of its episodes, gives it a particular historical value and at the same time a terrible pathos. Writer and reader were at the first night of the drama, watching the first act. There was no one to tell them what was going to happen before the fall of the last curtain.

When one sees that distant audience passionately watching the first act, one is agonizingly aware of what seems a strange naïveté, a dreadful unawareness of what they were about to receive. Thus the author, in mid-1917, wrote a brief note as preface to *Carrying On with the First Hundred Thousand*, a sequel produced in response to the immense popularity of the first book. (It had had a large success in the United States, too, and the author had been snatched from the Front and sent on a propaganda tour of the U.S.A.)

'*The First Hundred Thousand*', he wrote, 'closed with the battle of Loos. The present narrative follows certain friends of ours from the scene of that costly but valuable experience . . . to profitable participation in the Battle of the Somme.'

'Much has happened since then. The initiative has passed once and for all into our hands; so has the command of the air. Russia has been reborn, and like most healthy infants is passing through an uproarious period of teething trouble [i.e. the period between the abdication of the Tzar and the Bolshevik seizure of power]. But America has stepped in, and promises to do more than redress the balance. All along the Western Front we have begun to move forward without haste or flurry.'

A strangely similar, similarly eerie sensation is conveyed by an author who could be called the naval counterpart of Ian Hay. This was the officer who, under the pen-name 'Bartimeus', wrote immensely popular 'fictionalized reportage' about the war at sea, much of it also published in *Blackwood's*, and collected in book form under such titles as *Naval Occasions*, *A Tall Ship* and *The Long Trick*.

The last of these three was published in October 1917 and went into its fourth edition before the end of the year. Its climax is a vivid and, in detail, hideously realistic account of the Battle of Jutland – the first and last encounter between the

main naval forces of Britain and Germany. 'Such', wrote Bartimeus, 'was the Battle of the mist, a triumphant assertion,
after nearly two years of vigil and waiting, of British Sea Power.'
(It was so at least in the sense that in terms of tonnage and
gun-power the British had a superiority of approximately seven
to four. Much later critics of writers like Bartimeus treated this
fact as though it somehow detracted from the courage, tough-
ness, and ability of the British sailors, which is as nonsensical as
it would be to impugn the soldiers under Montgomery's command because he insisted on certain degrees of superiority in
numbers and fire-power.)
   The battle, Bartimeus continued,

'commenced with a cloud of smoke on the horizon no larger
than a man's hand. Its consequences and effects spread out
in widening ripples through space and time, changing the
vast policies of nations, engulfing thousands of humble lives,
and hopes and destinies. Centuries hence the ripples will still
be washing up the flotsam of that fight on the shores of
human life. Long after the last survivor has passed to dust the
echo of the British and German guns will rumble in ears
not yet conceived. Princes will hear it in the chimes of their
marriage bells; it will accompany the scratching of diplo-
matists' pens and the creaking wheels of the pioneer's ox-
wagon. It will sound above the clatter of Baltic shipyards and
in the silence of the desert where the caravan routes stretch
white beneath the moon. The Afghan, bending knife in hand
over a whetstone, and the Chinese coolie knee-deep in his
wet paddy-fields, will pause in their work to listen to the
sound, uncomprehending, even while the dust is gathering on
the labours of the historian and the novelist.'

Enflamed in 1917 by patriotic enthusiasm, misinformation,
and a general conviction that the North Sea was the centre of
the world, Bartimeus would have been astounded to read the
estimate of the Battle of Jutland published in the first post-war
volumes of the *Encyclopaedia Britannica*. 'The battle', writes the
Britannica coldly, 'was not a decisive one and the British battle
fleet [as distinct from the battle-cruiser squadrons] was never
seriously under fire. It must be admitted that the British
C.-in-C.'s tactics were characterized by excessive caution . . .

From one point of view it may be said that the result was successful ... But the battle of Jutland, taken by itself, must rank merely as a great and unique opportunity for the British fleet, of which advantage was not sufficiently taken.'

These parallel best-sellers, Hay for the land forces, Bartimeus for the navy, varied somewhat in their estimate of what was the suitable view to take of the German enemy. Of the two, Bartimeus was the more forthright. In his book the Germans were murderers of women and children, looters, and cowards. He offers a close-up of a submarine commander called von Sperrgebiet. He is told of British firing at his periscope. Immediately 'his face was white, and his lip curled back in a perpetual snarl like a wolf at bay ... His laugh was like the bark of a sick dog.'

Revealing enough of what the public, or a section of it, wanted to read, is von Sperrgebiet's supposed view of the English.

'He had always hated the English, even in his youth when for a year he occupied an inconspicuous niche in one of the less fastidious Public Schools. [It is here taken, most mistakenly, for granted that "fastidious" Public Schools, such as Eton, barred Germans.] He hated them for the qualities he despised and found so utterly inexplicable ... He despised their quixotic sense of justice and fairness in a losing game ... He despised their whole-hearted passion for sports at an age when he was beginning to be interested in less wholesome and far more complex absorptions. [As every British schoolboy knew, there was no sex at all, even at an unfastidious Public School.] He despised their straight, clean affections ... their shy, rather knightly mental attitude towards their sisters and one another's sisters ... But he also hated them for something he had never even admitted to himself. Crudely put, it was because he knew that he could never beat an Englishman. There was nothing in his spirit that could outlast the terrible, emotionless determination in the English character to win.'

In October 1917, when that was published, it was a solace to the readers to know that even the German officers already knew they could not win – even though they might not yet be admitting it to themselves. As a morale up-keeper, Bartimeus was doing well.

Ian Hay, reporting from Flanders, was rather more temperate in estimating the character of 'brother Boche'. Admittedly he was a sneaky, dirty sort of fighter, unlike the Boer – 'an adversary who was a gentleman'. (During the Boer War itself, the Boer had not been regarded as gentlemanly. He became so when viewed through the mists of time.) But what was really wrong with the Boche, and why he was doomed to failure, was his ridiculously methodical, regimented way of doing things, his lack of individual initiative. This was what was going to lose him command of the air.

'The average Boche [notes Hay's Colonel Wagstaffe] does not take kindly to flying. It is too – too individualistic a job for him. He likes to work in a bunch with other Boches, where he can keep step, and maintain dressing, and mark time if he gets confused. In the air one cannot mark time, and it worries Fritz to death.'

(In this connection some may recall reading, during the Second World War, the comforting news that the Japanese were no good in the air for similar reasons. They had the additional disadvantage of having something wrong with their ears, the result of being carried as babies on their mothers' backs. Thus as adult airmen they had no sense of direction.)

Possibly awareness of a low shock-level in their particular public inhibited these authors from suggesting that the Hun, in addition to being no gentleman and lacking individuality, was also, likely as not, a sodomite. The charge may have been made in other wartime best-sellers. I have come across it only in John Buchan's magnificent *Greenmantle*. There, when Major Hannay, disguised as a dissident South African, is taken by gross Junker von Stumm to his Bavarian castle, Hannay detects an air of effeminacy about von Stumm's private apartments. Yet he is sure they had not been touched by a woman's hand. He is then reminded of 'certain practices said to be not unknown in the German Army'.

Partly, no doubt, because Kitchener's First Army was Ian Hay's first close and continuous contact with the working class, his views on the political scene at the outbreak of war, and as he expects it to be when war is over, are particularly vivid and

sociologically valuable. Ventriloquizing, so to speak, the opinions
of early working-class volunteers from 'red' Clydebank, he writes
with faintly patronizing sarcasm :

> 'At home we are persons of some consequence, and with
> very definite notions about the dignity of labour. We have
> employers who tremble at our frown; we have Trades Union
> officials who are at constant pains to impress upon us our
> own omnipotence in the industrial world in which we live.
> We have at our beck and call a Radical M.P. who, in return
> for our vote and suffrage, informs us that we are the back-
> bone of the nation, and that we must on no account permit
> ourselves to be trampled upon by the effete and tyrannical
> upper classes.'

This was an accurate summary of the way the alarmed middle
class and the Conservative politicals saw the situation of the
working class during the near-revolutionary turmoil of the decade
before 1914. Ian Hay has good news for them. From the very
beginning of the international conflict, many of them had seen it
as at least a blessed escape from the class war. Through the
microcosm of Kitchener's Army Hay is able to confirm those
hopes. 'We realize that the Army is not, after all, as we first
suspected, divided into two classes – oppressors and oppressed.
We all have to "go through it" . . . Fresh air, hard training and
clean living begin to weave their spell.'

The spirit of class war is exorcized, and a little later Colonel
Wagstaffe, seen as a particularly clear-sighted man, is quoted as
saying, 'If the present scrap can only be prolonged for another
year, our country will receive a tonic which will carry it on for
another century . . . There is one thing worse than a long war
and that is a long peace.'

As is known, Major Wagstaffe's wish for prolongation of
the war was amply granted.

Somewhat later, this same Wagstaffe, brooding on what may
be expected to happen after the war, remarks comfortingly to
a younger officer that 'we are all going to understand one
another a great deal better after this war.'

   ' "Who? Labour and Capital, and so on?"'

"Labour and Capital is a meaningless and misleading expression. With the coming of peace this country will be invaded by several million of the wisest men that she has ever produced – the New British Army. That Army will consist of men who have spent three years [nearly four and a half as things turned out] in getting rid of mutual misapprehensions and assimilating one another's point of view ... They will flood this old country, and they will make short work of the agitator and the alarmist and the profiteer." '

The war was thus to bring about not merely a welcome interlude in the class war, but its miraculous cessation. Across the trench lines innumerable German officers shared the view of Major Wagstaffe. The returning army would wipe agitators and profiteers from the soil of Germany.

Luckily for Major Wagstaffe he could not preview that postwar edition of the *Encyclopaedia Britannica* already quoted.

'Within a few days of the Armistice deputations from workers, especially munition workers, were demanding of the Prime Minister a living wage. The railwaymen decided to withdraw the truce in their industry and demanded an eight-hour day, which the Government promptly conceded. Demobilised soldiers, miners, police, boiler-makers, dock workers, engineers, all made urgent demands, with strikes declared or threatened. At first the trouble was worse on the Clyde, but the outlook was soon gloomier in London ... The London electricians threatened to cut off all electricity if the Government did not settle with the Clyde workers. The Government met the threat by a regulation under the Defence of the Realm Act making electrical strikers liable to six months imprisonment.'

Egad!

IT IS CONVENIENT to quote here from my re-
miniscences of my maternal uncle, Philip Stephenson, a middle-
weight romantic novelist of the Edwardian and early Georgian
age. People, I recalled, told Uncle Philip that if he would
employ his notable gift of the conversational gab in a practical
manner, write the stuff instead of talking it, he would make a
fortune, like Stanley Weyman. People really did say that sort
of thing to articulate literate men at that time. I continued :

> 'It seemed a good idea, and, while waiting for the Calcutta
> sweep to pay off, he wrote and published at the rate of about
> one a year a number of historical romances. They included
> novels entitled *Love in Armour*, *A Gendarme of the King*,
> *The Black Cuirassier*, and *A Rose of Dauphiny*. It was un-
> fortunate from a financial point of view that he had a loving
> reverence for French history which he supposed the library
> subscribers shared. The historical details of his stories were
> to him both fascinating and sacred. He refused to adjust by
> a hair's breadth, in aid of suspense, romance or pace of action,
> anything whatever from an arquebus to a cardinal's mistress.
> Once you were past the title, you were on a conducted tour
> of a somewhat chilly and overcrowded museum.'

I mention this uncle of mine not because he had any great
importance in the literature of this period, nor because his novels
were fairly widely read and brought him in a reasonable income
year by year. I do so because he has to my mind a double
significance. In the late nineties he wrote two books, one of
which was called *How the Jubilee Fleet Escaped Destruction*.
The point of these books was to excite, by fictional means, the
supposedly indifferent or sluggish British public to a realization
that at any moment war with France might break out.

M. Halévy, in his brilliant history of British political life at this period (*A History of the English People in the Nineteenth Century*, 1924), mentions Philip Stephenson as indicative of a trend. Those books sold well. But soon it became evident that the impending Franco-British war was either not going to take place, or, even were it going to take place, was not engaging the attention of the British public by its imminence.

The fact that people held up Stanley Weyman to my uncle as an example was no accident. Stanley Weyman was the most accomplished as well as the most successful producer of what were sometimes called 'Cloak and Dagger' novels, and sometimes 'Wig and Powder' novels. They fell under the general heading of Historical Romances. We come here immediately on a curious paradox, which is exemplified by Stanley Weyman's books. On the one hand he clearly understood that the public, that is to say, people who were able to buy books or subscribe to the lending libraries, were curiously fascinated by past historical periods. Probably he knew that the France of the seventeenth or sixteenth century as envisaged by the library public in Britain of the early twentieth century had never existed. Just how the British public image of past centuries came into being is a matter of fascinating speculation. Why, for instance, are the Wars of the Roses romantic? Why are the bloody savageries and enormous political implications of the Civil War also romantic? Or rather why were they romantic to the public of, let us say, 1910? It would be easy to reply that it must have been the result of British public-school education. Nobody today thinks for instance that the Charge of the Light Brigade was otherwise than a tragic and disastrous affair throwing a frightful light upon the organization of the British Army, and the inadequate personalities of almost everyone concerned in the High Command. Yet Tennyson's poem managed to obliterate this image in the minds of hundreds of thousands of schoolboys, both at the time and for generations afterwards. How all those things came to pass would be a question that it would be interesting to answer if the historians could find out what the answer really is.

All that can be said here is that Stanley Weyman's public did have an entirely unrealistic and romantic view of the France of the sixteenth and seventeenth centuries. One could here of course use the word 'Escapism'. But this is in a sense a shorthand

word. What exactly does it mean? Escape from what to
what? One can only accept the fact. It was as I say a fact of
which Weyman took full advantage. But despite this Weyman,
once he had got all his characters on scene in the chosen century,
caused them to act realistically. He took the most laborious care
to see that his characters were credible as human beings, and
not as pasteboard figures passing through some charade of a
past age in which what seems incredible in the twentieth century
could be credibly enacted.

In other words, when Weyman presented a character as poor
and imperilled, he took pains to convince the readers that the
man really was poor, and really was in danger. Naturally since
the book is written in the first person we know that the 'Gentleman of France' won through in the end to prosperity and successful love. What I mean by referring to the realism of Weyman
is that there are long passages in the book in which, through the
skill of the writer, the reader is genuinely impressed by the
precariousness of the man's situation. Anyone who has ever
been in poverty or danger can identify temporarily with that
man. Evidently what the people of Weyman's day wanted was
a kind of escape into an imaginary historical world, but at the
same time a degree of realism once one was inside that world.

I emphasize these particular qualities of Stanley Weyman
(and they were the qualities also of lesser writers than he) because
there came a point when this type of realism although still
fairly popular was overtaken by demand for what an art critic
might describe as neo-non-realism. As usual it is impossible to
draw a firm line marking the time at which this change occurred.
One can only record the fact that it was in 1910 that Jeffery
Farnol published his first book, *The Broad Highway*. This book
was a bestseller from the start, sold tens of thousands over
several decades, and, significantly, has recently been re-
published in paperback by Pan Books. Jeffery Farnol owed, I
should suppose, a good deal to Stanley Weyman, just as I would
equally suppose that Georgette Heyer owes a good deal to
Jeffery Farnol.

There is no knowing at this time to what extent Jeffery Farnol
realized that his book was a breakaway from a partially realistic
tradition of historical romance. And one may feel perfectly certain that he would have been disgusted by the pomposity of such a
description as I have given him : namely that of a neo-non-realist.

In this kind of comparison one always risks appearing to be uttering some kind of literary judgement. One is assumed to be saying that, let us say, the realism of Stanley Weyman was 'better' than the non-realism of Jeffery Farnol. Naturally everyone may have his subjective opinions about that and may draw his conclusions about the people who preferred one writer to the other. Considerations of 'literary merit' must here be set aside. All that is being said is that at one point a certain realism was demanded even in historical romances and that at another point this particular demand ceased and was succeeded by the demand for total non-realism. Pushing the problem a little harder, one might remark that to some extent Jeffery Farnol's approach displayed an early understanding of Brecht's famous Alienation Effect. He seemed to be taking special care to inform the reader that this was a novel, a work of fiction, a contrivance. He was at pains to point out how the ingredients of the final brew were mixed. What Farnol calls the 'Antescriptum' to *The Broad Highway* makes this point very clear. It is supposed to be written by the fictional narrator of the story, Peter Vibart.

'As I sat of an early summer morning in the shade of a tree, eating fried bacon with a Tinker, the thought came to me that I might some day write a book of my own; a book that should treat of the roads and byroads, of trees, and wind and lonely places, of rapid brooks and lazy streams, of the glory of dawn, the glow of evening and the purple solitude of night; a book of wayside inns and sequestered taverns; a book of country things and ways and people. And the thought pleased me much.

"But," objected the Tinker, for I had spoken my thought aloud, "trees and suchlike don't sound very interesting least-ways not in a book, for after all a tree is only a tree and an inn an inn; no, you must tell of other things as well."

"Yes," I said, "to be sure there is a highwayman."

"Come, that's better," said the Tinker encouragingly.

"Then," I went on, ticking off each item on my fingers, "come Tom Cragg the pugilist . . ."

"Better and better," nodded the Tinker.

"A one-legged soldier of the peninsula, an adventure at a lonely tavern, a flight through woods at midnight pursued

by desperate villains, and a most extraordinary Tinker. So far
so good, I think, and it all sounds adventurous enough."

"Ah," said the Tinker, "I never read a novel with a Tinker
in it as I remember, they are generally dooks or earls or barro-
nits – nobody wants to read about a Tinker."

"That all depends," said I, "a Tinker may be much more
interesting than an Earl or even a Duke."

The Tinker examined the piece of bacon upon his knife
point with a cold and disparaging eye.

"I have read a good many novels in my time," he said,
shaking his head, "and I know what I am talking of." Here
he bolted the morsel of bacon with much apparent relish.
"I have made love to Duchesses, run off with Heiresses and
fought dooks – ah! by the hundred – all because of some book
or other, and enjoyed it uncommonly well, especially the
dooels. If you can get a bit of blood into your book, so much
the better, there's nothing like a little blood in a book – not
a great deal, but just enough to give it a tang so to speak:
If you could kill your highwayman to start with it would
be a very good beginning to your story."

"I could do that certainly," said I, "but it would not be
according to fact."

"So much the better," said the Tinker, "who wants fact in
a novel?"

"Hum," said I.

"And then again . . ."

"What more?" I enquired.

"Love," said the Tinker, wiping his knife blade on the
leg of his breeches.

"Love?" I repeated.

"And plenty of it," said the Tinker.

"I am afraid that is impossible," said I after a moment's
thought.

"How impossible?"

"Because I know nothing about love."

"That's a pity," said the Tinker.

"Under the circumstances, it is," said I . . .

"Young fellow," said he, "no man can write a good novel
without he knows something about love, it aren't to be expected, so the sooner you do learn the better."

"Hum," said I.

"I say it again, they want love in a book nowadays, and what is more they will have it ... What you have to do is to give them a little blood now and then with plenty of love and you can't go far wrong."

Now whether the Tinker's theory on the writing of a good novel be right or wrong I will not presume to say. But in this book that lies before you, though you shall read if you choose of country things and ways and people, yet because that part of my life herein recorded was a something hard rough life, you shall read also of blood; and because I came in the end to love very greatly, so shall you read of love.

Wherefore then I am emboldened to hope that when you shall have turned the last page and closed this book, you shall do so with a sigh.'

To attempt to summarize the plot of a Farnol novel, or rather to suggest that such a summary conveys more than a whiff of the essential smell of the novel itself, is as unfair as to attempt to encapsulate the plot of a musical which has the audience humming in their seats. Farnol certainly knew how to make them hum and has kept them humming ever since. Still a sketch of the Farnol type of plot is of some importance as indicating how little either Farnol or his readers bothered about the loud creaking of the machinery. It may be imagined that Stanley Weyman and his readers would have considered a Farnol plot as being blatantly, almost insultingly, 'contrived'. *The Broad Highway*, for instance, opens with the reading of the will of George Vibart, which concerns his two nephews Maurice and Peter. 'Moreover the sum of £500,000, now vested in the funds, shall be paid to either Maurice or Peter Vibart aforesaid if either shall within one calendar year become the husband of the Lady Sophia Sefton of Cambourne.'

Neatly displayed in the first chapter, like advertisements of melodrama to come, are the following facts: The Lady Sophia is 'a reigning toast'. She is 'the most famous beauty in the country, London's mad over her – she can pick and choose from all the finest gentlemen in England.' She is also said to have galloped her horse up the steps of St Paul's Cathedral and down again. 'She is none of your milk and watery meek-mouthed misses – curse me no! She is all fire and blood and high metal – a woman sir, glorious – divine – damme, sir, a black-browed

goddess – a positive plum!' Regarding Maurice Vibart:
' "Egad!" cried Sir Richard, "Who hasn't heard of Buck
Vibart – beat Ted Jarraway of Swansea in five rounds – drove
coach and four down Whitehall on sidewalk— ran away with a
French Marquise while but a boy of twenty, and shot her husband into the bargain. Devilish celebrated figure in sporting
circles, friend of the Prince Regent." '

Of Peter Vibart we learn that he is a scholarly young man
who has some athletic achievement to his credit, has completed
a new and original translation of Quintilian, and another of
Petronius, but has no knowledge of the world outside Oxford
University. He is also penniless. Apart from the clause in the
will relating to the possible marriage to Lady Sophia, Uncle
George has bequeathed to Peter nothing but his blessing and the
sum of ten guineas in cash. To cousin Maurice on the other
hand he bequeathed the sum of twenty thousand pounds 'in the
fervent hope that it may help him to the devil within the year
or as soon after as may be'.

Another uncle, Sir Richard, and the lawyer who has just
read the will enquire what Peter proposes to do when his money
is all gone. He replies that he will turn his hand to some useful
employment, 'digging, for instance'.

'Digging!' ejaculated Sir Richard, 'and you a scholar – and
what is more, a gentleman!'

Peter's reply is of interest since it expresses sentiments sharply
different from those usually uttered by the heroes of historical
romances of that period, and comes near to infringing some of
the taboos ordinarily respected by the authors. Jeffery Farnol,
although born and brought up in England, went from the Westminster Art School to America at the age of twenty and it was
while a scene-painter at the Astor Theater in New York that
he wrote *The Broad Highway*. (It was rejected by American
publishers as being too English.) It could be that his plunge
into the relatively astringent atmosphere of the New York of that
period was responsible for his fortunate escape from some of the
conventions which hemmed in his contemporaries.

' "My dear Sir Richard," said I, "that all depends upon
how you would define a gentleman. To me he would appear
of late years to have degenerated into a creature whose chief
end in life is to spend money he has never earned, to

reproduce his species with a deplorable frequency and promis-
cuity, to drink more than is good for him, and, between
whiles, to fill in his time hunting, cock-fighting, or watching
entranced while two men pound each other unrecognisable
in the prize ring. Occasionally he has the good taste to break
his neck in the hunting field, or get himself gloriously shot
in a duel, but the generality live on to a good old age, turn
their attention to matters political and, following the dictates
of their class, damn all reform with a whole-hearted fervour
equalled only by their rancour."

"Deuce take me!" ejaculated Sir Richard feebly, while
Mr Grainger buried his face in his pocket handkerchief.

"To my mind the man who sweats over a spade or follows
the tail of a plough is far nobler and higher in the Scheme
of Things than any of your young bloods driving his coach
and four to Brighton to the danger of all and sundry."

Sir Richard slowly got up out of his chair, staring at me
open mouthed. "Good God!" he exclaimed at last, "the boy
is a Revolutionary!" '

In fourteen pages, including the 'Antescriptum', the plot has
been hammered together in full view of the reader, and the
entire contraption is now ready to push off. To change the
metaphor, Farnol has in those pages very deliberately tele-
graphed his punches. No reader can be in much doubt that
Peter Vibart, after some blood-letting and some adversity, is
going to encounter and ultimately marry the Lady Sophia. In
other words, the element of 'suspense' has been virtually eliminated. (It should perhaps be said that the only 'surprise', if it
can so be called, is that in the course of the story the fact emerges
that the two cousins, the Good and the Bad, are physically
almost identical, so that the Good Peter is repeatedly mistaken
for the Bad Maurice, with results sometimes beneficial, sometimes perilous to himself.) No reader has to waste a minute
wondering how it is all going to come out and not more than a
minute and a half at any point in the story wondering what is
going to happen next. What is going to happen next is comfortably predictable. The 'surprises' are cunningly sprung in such
a way that the reader has foreseen what is to come before he
gets there. The interest of the reader therefore has to be engaged,
and is successfully engaged, almost entirely by the vividness of

Farnol's descriptions of scenes of violence interspersed with scenes of rural beauty, of restrained passages of *l'amour* (complicated by fearful misunderstandings as to the relative social status of those concerned), and encounters with philosophic figures. It would have been reasonable for Farnol's first publisher to have blenched at the absence of suspense. He could have seen it as the possible ruin of the book's chances in the market. By hindsight we know that he would have been wrong. In reality the absence of suspense was a positive asset to the book.

On this point there are two things to be said. First, as Farnol must have realized when he wrote his 'Antescriptum,' non-suspense is a sedative for people who need to be sedated. It used to be, indeed it still is, widely believed by many people that the period between the end of the Boer War and the outbreak of the First World War was a patch of English History resembling, at least so far as the middle class was concerned, the Garden of Eden, and the adjective most constantly applied to those days is 'halcyon'. The notion was of course fostered by people looking back at the 'halcyon days' from the murk of 1925. The discomforts of the present produced a nostalgia for a largely imaginary past. It may be true that the middle class of 1910 was materially more comfortable than in 1925. By inference it is supposed that its members enjoyed a sense of complacent security. It is also possible that for a few years their lives really may have been more secure than in the post-war years. But the point is not the true relative difference between their status in 1910 and in 1925, but what they supposed their status to be. And most of the evidence points to the fact that most of them did not feel secure at all. There were war scares at least once a year. On the home front they faced unprecedented industrial upheaval. They are frequently represented as dim-witted fools dancing on the slopes of the well-known volcano which was shortly to erupt. Naturally they had slender means of foreseeing with certainty the outbreak of the war of 1914. Even those who did could not conceivably have had any prevision of the real horror to come. It is true that they grasped eagerly at the theories produced by economists and others suggesting that a world war was impossible under the conditions of modern industrial civilization, because the great financial powers and other authorities of the world would realize that such a war would be ruinous. Even if it were to break out it would inevitably grind to a halt within a few months for lack of money or credit. These beliefs are often treated as matter for satire. The middle-class public of the period is seen as in the main a collection of complacently fat-headed vulgarians who had no notion of what was just about to happen. No doubt there were as many vulgar fools on hand as at any given period of history. But the eagerness at which they grasped at straws showing that the wind was blowing against war can be interpreted with equal reasonableness in the opposite way. It could mean that they were so sharply aware of a possible disaster that they were certainly not going to neglect any pronouncement by a *savant* giving hope that the disaster might after all be averted.

To people living in such circumstances, a technique which soothingly eliminated suspense was an evident boon. And Farnol's technique in this respect showed a profound understanding of what was needed. The cunning of the author's 'Antescriptum' consisted in the fact that it in effect assured the reader that the swords were only property swords, that the blood was not real blood, that only the really bad would get murdered, and that the hero, despite a well-staged sham fight with adversity here and there, would in the end win the hand of as physically and spiritually lovely a lass as an English gentleman could wish to meet. However shrilly the winds of reality might blow outside, the reader who embarked on the good ship Farnol could be certain of a brilliantly sunlit cruise right through to the last paragraph :

'And thus did I, all unworthy as I am, win the heart of a noble woman whose love I pray will endure, even as mine will, when we shall have journeyed to the end of this Broad Highway, which is Life, and into the mystery of the Beyond.'

The other matter arising in connection with this question of suspense or the absence of it is of a rather more general character. We may take a line through the Greek dramatists. The plays of Aeschylus, Sophocles, and Euripides were firmly, sometimes rigidly, based upon myths which were the common heritage and common knowledge of the citizens in the audience. There was no question of any serious deviation from the 'story-line' of the myth. In this respect the plays were the total antithesis of the Whodunnit. This absence of suspense was a feature of the Greek drama which distinguished it from most Western drama of the centuries since the Middle Ages.

In the Middle Ages drama was based upon the commonly known Christian story, or on other Biblical myths such as the story of Adam and Eve. At that time everyone had a pretty good idea what that serpent was up to. In Athens everyone knew who murdered or was going to murder Agamemnon. Everyone knew that Oedipus was going to kill his father and marry his mother. Nobody was sitting agape in the audience waiting for the moment when someone would rush on stage shouting, 'Don't marry her, she's your mum!' In the absence of a sufficiency of commonly accepted myths of this calibre, the Western world had to invent, so to speak, makeshift myths from time to time. An obvious case in point is the traditional 'Western'. (Of recent years this particular myth has been exploded or fragmented, partly by normal wear and tear, partly by a new political and social awareness of what the whites really did to the Indians.) There have been others. In connection with Stanley Weyman I have already mentioned the myth of French history, which was again brilliantly exploited – and I use the word 'exploited' in no pejorative sense – by Georgette Heyer in, for example, *The Old Shades*, a book which was first published in 1926, went on selling like ice-cream for three decades, was published in a new edition in 1956, and reprinted nine times between 1962 and 1969.

In the field of romance, Georgian England from roughly the first Jacobite rising of 1715 to the period of the Regency has provided a very durable myth. (I hope it may be otiose to emphasize that the word 'myth', which is a good deal misused, is not here to be taken as the equivalent of 'invention', 'fantasy', or 'lie'.) The question as to what extent a given novelist presented a false or distorted picture of a period, the extent to which a novel of this kind is a sort of *montage*, rather than anything in the nature of a documentary, is irrelevant. The existence of the myth is important, and indeed essential, because it provides a background, framework, and atmosphere which is understood, accepted, and indeed expected by a wide range of readers.

In a romance set in the period of England under the Georges we know that there are likely to be rather more Bucks and Bullies to the square mile than probably existed in reality. Their density in relation to the total population is expected to be very

high. The same is true of heiresses in distress. The list of properties indispensable to a Georgian romance is a long one. The
publishers' blurbs of the latest editions of some of these romances
demonstrate clearly the nature of the myth. Of *The Broad
Highway* the publishers note : 'Set amid the lovely countryside
of Kent, the glorious days of the Regency come vividly alive
in Jeffery Farnol's famous novel.' 'Glorious' is here the operative
word. Since we are dealing with a myth it would be ludicrous,
not to say curmudgeonly, to snoop around that word demanding
to know just how glorious these days were, and glorious for
whom. That sort of reality has nothing to do with the myth.
Leaping over twenty years and a World War, we reach the
publication-date in 1930 of Hugh Walpole's *Rogue Herries*. This
book, says its latest publisher, 'mirrors the heart and pulse of
eighteenth-century England'.

> 'Here is fiction in glorious sweeping measure, set against
> the wild and beautiful scenery of the Lake District, crowded
> with fairs, balls, weddings, duels, rebels, witches, abductions,
> murder, strolling players, and Jacobite agents.
>
> Bestriding these events like a colossus is proud, intolerant
> Francis Herries – the Dark Angel of Borrowdale – who des-
> pised his wife and sold his mistress at a public fair, yet came
> to love sixteen-year-old Mirabelle Starr more than life itself.'

J. B. Priestley gave the book his accolade as a 'superb work
of fiction'; so that just as *When It Was Dark* came to the public
with the blessing of the Bishop of London, the buyers and
borrowers of the books were assured that in *Rogue Herries* they
had an absolutely O.K. read. Observers who imagined that the
great depression of the thirties and the outbreak of the Second
World War would spoil the market for this kind of literature
were shown to be superficial in their judgements.

Rogue Herries and other volumes of *The Herries Chronicle*,
described by the *Daily Telegraph* as 'one of the great literary
triumphs of our time', went on selling strongly through all the
Sturm und Drang years and the latest edition was published by
Pan Books in 1971. It would be captious not to say narking, to
enquire the titles of the other 'great literary triumphs of our
time'. Nor, in emphasizing the mythical aspect, am I to be supposed to ignore the fact that though many thousands of readers

must have been captivated by Walpole's literary style *per se*. There are others who would probably prefer the relatively wind-less, figuratively speaking, heaths of his first successful and entirely unromantic novel – concerned with a feud between masters in an English private school – published before the First World War and entitled *Mr Perrin and Mr Traill*. It shocked people at the time with its strong homosexual undertones and with its only slightly muted suggestions that there was something rotten in the state of the British educational system.

Nobody was likely to be shocked by *The Herries Chronicle*. On the one hand, any reasonably experienced reader of romances could tell after a quick flutter in the bookshop or library that this was essentially a reliable exposition of the Georgian myth. They could do so even without benefit of the blurb to the latest edition which I have just quoted.

The conventions of the Georgian myth are soothing and sedative in the sense that they serve to place the action of the story at a certain distance from reality. Here a misunderstanding is possible. The 'distance from reality' is not to be measured in terms of calendar years. It depends on the extent to which the period chosen is deliberately and acceptably mythical. One may consider, for example, Tolstoy and Oliver Onions. The 1812 of Tolstoy is only 'mythical' in the sense that the Napoleonic invasion was already part of an accepted European saga. In every other respect its realism is timeless. Oliver Onions' *The Story of Ragged Robyn* (written and published in 1945 when the author was seventy-two years old and a near bestseller at the time, re-published by Penguin Books in 1954) is set in the late seventeenth century. The period is not one of the fully recognized 'myth reserves' of English history. But in any case *The Story of Ragged Robyn* contains no mythical element at all. There are knives and pistols but they are not property knives and pistols; they cut. The protection racketeers operating on the East Coast of England seem as genuinely daunting as any gang of protection racketeers in Los Angeles or Soho today. The hero's final triumph and tragedy are rendered by the author's imagination and mastery of narrative, simultaneously as startling as a thundercloud and as inevitable as doomsday. Small wonder that John Betjeman said of this book: 'Such a feeling of remoteness, boding inevitability, horror, such a sense of the past and such narrative power, are rarely to be found in one book.' And a B.B.C. critic rightly remarked that 'When I hear this or that writer acclaimed as the best living English Novelist, I feel inclined to put in a word for Oliver Onions.' The relevance here of *The Story of Ragged Robyn* is not that it is an exceptionally fine book, which it is. It is relevant to the discussion of what one may call the orthodox bestsellers in the field of historical romance precisely by reason of the gigantic contrast to them which it offers. By its total indifference to the conventional mythology of the historical romance it helps to illuminate the mythology itself.

Although twenty years elapsed between the publication of *The Broad Highway* and that of *Rogue Herries*, the romance based on the Georgian myth did not languish meanwhile. Thus, about midway between those two dates was published Warwick Deeping's *Apples of Gold*. Once again the blurb is instructive. After all, the publisher knows, or is supposed to know, what features of the book ought to be brought most prominently to the attention of the reader. The blurb to the latest edition of *Apples of Gold* reads:

> '*Apples of Gold* is a story of London. Or to be a little more accurate about both time and place, it is a story set in and around Covent Garden between 1715 and 1725 when George II was King. But despite its title it is not a story about the market. Its hero is Jordan March, a fencing teacher who taught in a Fencing School in Covent Garden. The school, its clientele and their involvement in the Whig-Tory riots of the time form the basis of the story, but the adventures of Jordan March himself provide no little excitement and interest.
>
> He fights, flirts, speculates in the South Sea Bubble, and eventually marries the wrong girl. Deep in difficulties both marital and financial, he works hard to free himself from what he sees as the great adventure of his life – the Search for the Apples of Gold.'

In Warwick Deeping's book the percentage of Bucks and Bullies is approximately as high as in Farnol's *The Broad Highway*, and as in Farnol's book the fact that the athletic hero is also a man given to gravely reflective philosophizing on the meaning of life maintains the necessary thread between the historical myth and the mind of the modern reader. For in all such books it is the business of the hero by his sagacity, audacity, physical prowess, and a general derring-do, to provide anything that the imagination of the reading Walter Mitty has failed to provide by itself. *Apples of Gold* is sufficiently different in tone and treatment from *The Broad Highway* to be seen as just one typical example of how the skilled craftsman can manipulate his material. It can certainly be said that *Apples of Gold* is a great deal less 'contrived', less obviously rigged and more dependent on sustained suspense, than *The Broad Highway*. For a long time we really are not certain whether the hero is going to marry the desperately inhibited and ultimately shrewish English girl who was his first love, or the beautiful visiting widow from Virginia. The problem is solved in the last two pages with a degree of credibility which Jeffery Farnol would probably not have bothered to have achieved; or, more probably, he would have considered that such credibility could only be achieved at the cost of demanding from the reader an attention which he might well find wearisome. I have no intention of discussing here whether one of these books is 'better' than the other. What seems certain is that neither *The Broad Highway*, *Apples of Gold* nor *Rogue Herries* could have had the immediate appeal it did, had the Georgian myth not been there to be exploited.

In view of all this, it is no longer surprising that the middle-class reader should have been drawn to – should even have demanded – a long look at people and situations activated by some kind of moral and spiritual certainty, even by some kind of just intelligible religious fanaticism. And that phenomenon can be observed, reflecting the doubts and divisions of the middle class, in British literature throughout the first half of the twentieth century.

Long hard winter

THE TITLE WAS *If Winter Comes*. The book was published in August 1921, with the country shaking from the effects of the biggest coal strike since 1912. To the British economy, winter came sure enough, in a near-panic of financial freeze and squeeze. By Christmas, one of the few products of which sales were not slumping but booming like penicillin in a pneumonia epidemic was the novel by A. S. M. Hutchinson. Between the beginning of December and the New Year, Hodder and Stoughton brought out a record-breaking five editions, making ten since August, an average of one every fortnight. It was selling like a magazine. By March 1922 it had run to nineteen editions, with demand still strong.

'Old Puzzlehead' was the nickname of the hero. His outstanding quality, source of many of his troubles, was that he could always see both sides of a question. He could see what a lot there was to be said for socialists on the one hand and capitalists on the other. His head, getting metaphorically bloodier and bloodier, was ultimately unbowed. His noble visions of human life in general and English life in particular were ignored or derided by the sluggish, the crass, and the villainous. It would have been impossible to invent a hero with whom the British middle class of the period could more readily identify.

For the novelist seeking mass-appeal in the early nineteen-twenties, the First World War was a gift, a natural, manna from heaven. It furnished him with a range of fictional and dramatic equipment such as had been ready to hand in the workshops of the Greek classical dramatists. In the Athenians, these had an audience which shared a common knowledge of the principal myths and legends concerning gods and men.

In this sense, the First World War had, for the novelist, the essential qualities of a great myth. Its general story-line was familiar to all. It could be approached from any angle the writer

might choose, but a general knowledge of the basic material he
was using was common to everyone. Also it had a beginning, a
middle, and, within the vivid memory of all, an end. Like a myth,
too, it afforded full opportunity for the dramatic use of hindsight,
particularly ironic hindsight. If the Greek chorus or other characters at the beginning of the play thought Orestes was going to
live happily ever after, the audience had the grim thrill of knowing better. A similar chilling thrill could be produced in the
1920s by characters seen to be dancing, in 1912, on the edge of
the abyss, or announcing confidently in August 1914 that 'the
lads'll be out of the trenches by Christmas'. To read, in 1921,
of characters solemnly arguing ten years earlier about whether
war is or is not possible, and often coming to the conclusion that
it is not, was to feel oneself endowed with an almost divine pre-
science apt to bring a purr to the throat of the ego.

These advantages were most fully exploited both by Hutchinson and, in an oddly and significantly parallel bestseller published
in the same year, *Simon Called Peter*, by Robert Keable.
(Students writing theses on 'the inter-war mentality of the
British middle class' are recommended to study the two books
in conjunction.)

In a newsreel-type sequence reconstructing the supposed climate of opinion between 1912 and 1914, Hutchinson gives himself
and his readers the full benefit of ironic hindsight, but uses it to
appear to display a facetious contempt for the 'great public' in
general, and the popular newspapers in particular. For a moment
this attitude might seem paradoxical in a writer whose appeal
is directed towards that same great public, queueing up fortnightly at the bookshops and lending libraries for the latest
edition of *If Winter Comes*.

Not so.

The reader is intended to see himself in the hero, Mark Sabre,
and does so. And Sabre's long suit is that he sees beyond the
events which so excite, titillate or enflame the almost witless
masses all round. It is not pretended that pre-war Sabre knew
exactly what was going to happen next; it was just that he had
a wider vision of human problems, a deeper moral understanding
than did most of the others. This confirmed the post-war reader in
his opinion that he, *frère et semblable* to Sabre, was one of the
few people capable of seeing the truth about the industrial,
political, moral, and religious turmoil of 1921. Peter Graham,

curate turned Army chaplain and hero of Keable's book, had
the same noble if unpopular knack.

'In October 1913', Hutchinson writes, 'life was going along at
a most delirious and thrilling and entirely fascinating speed.
There never was such a delicious and exciting and progressive
year as between October, 1912 and October, 1913.' (Aha! little
did they know!)

> 'You never knew what splendid sensation was next in store
> for you in 1913; but there always was a splendid sensation,
> lashed into the most deliciously agonizing thrills by the Press;
> and mellowing them all, for those who thought tuppence about
> such trivialities, was the fact that international peace, like the
> rising sun among mists, began to dissipate the storm clouds
> which had burst over the Balkans and (so the scaremongers
> said) had threatened elsewhere ... Not that relations with
> Germany counted for anything in the whirl of intensely agree-
> able sensations of these excellent days.'

But, as his true love, well-born and nobly wed Lady Tybar
admiringly tells Sabre, 'You've got ideas. You're rather an ideary
person.' He is indeed. He has a lot more ideas than do the fellows
at the club or in his office (let alone his vulgarly Philistine shrew
of a wife) – about God, personal morality, and, especially, his
country. As early as the summer of 1912 he has started to write
a book about the latter.

He has a mass of 'thoughts and feelings' on the subject. 'The
title he had conceived alone stirred them in his mind and drew
them from his mind as a magnet stirs and draws iron filings.
"England". Just "England". He could see it printed and published and renowned as "Sabre's England" ... It was to be just
"England"; the English of the English people and how and why.
And the first sentence said so.'

The opening sentences Sabre fictionally wrote in 1912 were
well suited to uplift the spirits of those readers of 1921 who,
while not wishing to commit themselves, at a time of fierce industrial strife, to any particular policy or cause, yet needed to see
themselves amid the surrounding gloom as sturdy democrats
with a glorious heritage and equally glorious future. 'This
England', wrote Sabre, 'is *yours*. It belongs to *you*.'

'Many enemies have desired to take it, because it is the most
glorious and splendid country in the world. But they have
never taken it because it is *yours* and has been kept for *you* . . .
not by kings, or statesmen or great men alone, but by the
English people. Down the long years they have handed it on
to you, as a torch is sent from hand to hand, and you in your
turn will hand it on down the long years before you. They
made the flame of England bright and ever brighter for you;
and you, stepping into all that they have made for you, will
make it bright and brighter yet. They passed and are gone;
and you will pass and go. But England will continue. Your
England. *Yours.*'

When the hand of Hutchinson the craftsman wavers, Sabre is
in danger of becoming a mere incarnation of virtues such as
decency, intellectual honesty, and moral courage, which the
reader is persuaded – a bit more or a bit less according to his
suggestibility – that he shares with the hero. But the hand seldom
wavers. With loving skill Sabre is kept on the move simultaneously as a symbol and as a specific individual, susceptible of
change and development.

By early 1918, invalided out of the army with a game leg, he
suffers black doubts about the present and the future of England.
The country, he muses gloomily to his solicitor friend Hapgood,
has been high on the crest of the wave during the war,

'but when the peace comes you look out for the glide down
into the trough . . . Man, what can you see already? Temples
everywhere to a new God – Greed – Profit – Extortion . . . All
out to get the most and do the least . . . You'll get the people
finding there's a limit to the high prices they can demand for
their labour : apparently none to those the employers can go
on piling up for their profits. You'll get growing hatred by the
middle class with fixed incomes of the labouring classes whose
prices for their labour they'll see – and feel – going up and up;
and you'll get the same growing hatred by the labouring classes
for the capitalists . . . I tell you, Hapgood, the trough's ahead;
we're steering for it, and its rapid and perilous sundering of
the classes.'

'What's the remedy?' Hapgood asks hopefully.

Sabre the visionary then lets fly with the following:

'Hapgood, the remedy's the old remedy. The old God. But
it's more than that. It's Light: more Light ... We want a
new revelation in terms of the new world's understanding. We
want light! ... Do you suppose an age that knows wireless
and can fly is going to find spiritual sustenance in the food of an
age that thought thunder was God speaking? ... Plumb down
in the crypt and abyss of every man's soul is a hunger, a crav-
ing for other food than this earthy stuff. And the Churches
know it; and instead of reaching down to him what he wants
– light, light – they invite him to dancing and picture shows ...
and the padres come down and drink beer with him, and watch
boxing matches with him ... and dance Jazz with him and
call it making religion a Living Thing in the Lives of the
People ... A man wouldn't care *what* he had to give up if he
knew he was making for something inestimably precious. But
he doesn't know. Light, Light – that's what he wants, and the
longer it's with-held the lower he'll sink. Light! Light!'

Regrettably, the man to whom Hapgood reports Sabre's warnings and Sabre's solution seems unimpressed even by 'Light' with
a capital 'L'. He just 'sits there like a surfeited python'. Fortunately for Hutchinson and his publishers, this was evidently not the
general reaction. People read on eagerly, and a few pages later, a
month having past, found Sabre informing Hapgood that he's
'got the secret. I've got the key to the riddle that's been puzzling
me all my life. I've got the new revelation in terms good enough
for me to understand. Light, more light. Here it is: God – is
love.'

'Simon called Peter', in Keable's book, after a lot of soul-
searching and acute woman trouble, comes up with approximately the same explanation of everything. He gets his revelation
at breakfast-time in Westminster Cathedral where he has gone
for a breather before returning to his mistress's bed in what seems
to be the Piccadilly Hotel.

(Reading Keable one sometimes recalls the reaction of Nick,
narrator of *The Great Gatsby*. During a drinking party in New
York, 'I sat down discreetly in the living room and read a chapter
of *Simon Called Peter* – either it was terrible stuff, or the whisky
distorted things, because it didn't make sense to me.')

One gets from time to time the impression that really there had been no break with the world of de Vere Stacpoole, and that what hundreds of thousands of people were looking for was some blue lagoon of the soul.

Get around to women, and you find significantly closer parallels between 'Old Puzzlehead' and the soul-torn chaplain.

For instance, each is lumbered at the outset by a woman of the kind 'the world' thinks 'nice'. Sabre's wife Mabel is the only daughter of the Dean of Tidborough. Peter Graham's fiancée, Hilda, is described as 'the daughter of a big house in Park Lane' and her father is a rich city merchant, pillar of the fashionable church of St John's. In their different ways, both are nastily superficial, deaf to spiritual promptings, unaware that beyond worldly cares and worldly success there is 'something else', and therefore incapable of enduring, let alone assisting their high-thinking menfolk.

For the woman reader these coarse-grained bitches are there to provide opportunity for anti-identification. Every literate woman could see at once where Mabel and Hilda were so utterly inadequate, and know – in page after page – how much more 'understanding' she would have been in admittedly trying conditions. When Sabre, for the most impeccably compassionate reasons, insists on bringing the former hired help, 'little Effie', and her new-born illegitimate baby to live in the house, Mabel flounces out. And this though it is emphasized that Effie, despite being the daughter of a mere works foreman, is 'ladylike'. In like manner Hilda, learning from his letters that Peter, in search of light, is moving around among prostitutes and hard-drinking officers at base camps in Rouen and Le Havre, breaks off the engagement. She simply fails to understand a long letter he has written to her from France explaining what he thinks about Christ and sin, and concluding with the assurance, 'I mean to try and get down to reality myself, and try and weigh it up. I am going to eat and drink with publicans and sinners; maybe I shall find my Master still there.'

The news about the publicans and sinners goes down very badly in Park Lane.

But let none think that there are not good women and true in England. Peter Graham picks up a nurse (admittedly, and rather emphatically, a colonial from South Africa) who not only gives him a wonderful time in bed but in the end agonizedly

refuses to marry him because his love for her is going to interfere
with his love of God. The Frenchwomen in the story are mostly
prostitutes, but one of them has a heart of gold and gives Peter
much-needed sexual release. She hesitates because she thinks
he may be going to spoil everything by offering her money.

> ' "Forgive me dear," he muttered, "I thought you would
> help me to feel a man . . . I've a body, like other men. Let me
> plunge down deep tonight, Louise."
> Then did the girl of the streets set out to play her chosen
> part . . . If ever Magdalene broke an alabaster box of very
> precious ointment, Louise did so that night. She was worldly
> wise, and she did not disdain to use her wisdom.'

A few days later they drop in at a Mass together. The chaplain,
it appears, has never heard of the doctrine of the Real Presence.
Louise explains it to him in a few simple words. 'Peter all but
stopped in the road. It was absurd that so simple a thing should
have seemed to him new, but so it is with us all. "Jesus Himself!"
he exclaimed and broke off abruptly . . . He pulled himself together; it was too good to be true.'

Better than any of them is Sabre's Lady Tybar. They have
loved one another since childhood, but she marries the glamor-
ous, though morally evil, Lord Tybar instead. Meeting two years
later, she and Sabre fall in love all over again, for she is lovely
and he, as already stated, 'ideary'.

But his ideas and ideals prove a big impediment to their happiness. Just when Nona, Lady Tybar, seems all set to have an
affair with him, he gets off a longish spiel about why he is partly
against 'conventions' and at the same time absolutely for them.
(This is one of the characteristics that make it so easy for a
broad-minded yet essentially respectable English citizen to identify
with him. And even if the citizen's teenage children got their
hands on the book, it certainly would not turn them into reckless rebels.) 'Convention, you know, it's the most mysterious,
extraordinary thing. It's a code society has built up to protect
itself and to govern itself . . . All sorts of things that the law
doesn't give and couldn't give, our conventions shove in on us
in the most amazing way.'

Nora breaks in to declare that she thinks conventions 'odious',
'hateful'. But Sabre surges on.

' "Yes, yes, I know, odious, hateful and much more than that, cruel – conventions can be as cruel as hell. I was just coming to that. But they're all absolutely rightly based, Nona. That's the baffling and the maddening part of them. That's what interests me in them. In their application they're often unutterably wrong, cruel, hideously cruel and unjust, but when you examine them, even at their cruellest, you can't help seeing that they're absolutely right and reasonable and necessary."

Nona nodded. "I *do* think that's interesting, Marko. I think that's most awfully interesting." '

One conventional block to their happiness is removed when Lord Tybar, after getting the V.C., is killed at Arras. But Mabel remains. And what with her, and the war, and dreadful doubts about the Meaning of It All, and Effie's little baby (which people think is Sabre's though it is not), and being ostracized and thrown out of his job, and virtually accused of manslaughter when Effie kills the baby and commits suicide, Sabre experiences some very dark nights of the soul.

He speaks of the frightful things that have happened to him. He wants to 'get right away'.

But Nona is at hand. 'Marko,' she tells him, 'your dear England in those years suffered frightful things. She suffered lies, calumnies, hateful and terrible things – not in one little place, but across the world. Those who loved her trusted her, and she has come through those dark years; and those who know you have trusted you *always*, and you are coming through those days to show to all . . . Time, Marko; time heals all things, forgets all things, and proves all things.'

It seems possible that Noel Coward was influenced by this speech when writing the last act of *Cavalcade*. One may recall the contemporary satirist who wrote of that act how

> '. . . *the dowagers wept in the stalls,*
> *And I really can't see*
> *Why the man next to me*
> *Repeatedly said it was balls.*'

Encircling Sabre with her arms, Nona cries, 'You are never going to leave me, Marko. Never, never, never till death.'

With his habitual repetitiousness, which at this supreme moment seems to affect the author too, Sabre 'cried "Beloved, beloved" and clung to her. "Beloved, beloved!" and clung to her.'

He had found Light, Light, and they were married in 1919.

Stephen Sorrell of *Sorrell and Son* (first edition August 1925, fortieth edition February 1953) was a near-contemporary of Mark Sabre and shared many of his opinions, but was on the whole a more rugged character, his feet planted more securely on the soil of reality. Warwick Deeping, author also of *Apples of Gold*, was wholly concerned, as Hutchinson partially was, to present the plight of the Englishman returned from the First World War to face the England which had emerged from what long immersion in the pages of the bestsellers compels me to describe as 'the holocaust'.

Unlike Hutchinson, Deeping is at pains to present his hero not as a kind of odd-man-out, but as essentially the English *homme moyen sensuel*. The plot is anchored to a firm appreciation of the importance of class and class-distinction in England. It is essentially a study of the middle-class man threatened with submersion, indeed, for a time actually submersed, in the proletariat. In this lies its value as a document. I was about to write 'as distinct from its readability as a story'. But really one ought not to make that distinction. The document is the story. If thousands of people read it on its first publication, and thousands went on reading it up to that fortieth edition in 1953, then it must be that they found the author's view of the class position, and the resulting misfortunes of the middle-class man, both attractive and tolerable. In contrast to Sabre's liberal puzzle-headedness, these views are expressed forthrightly, sometimes in internal monologues by Sorrell himself, sometimes in conversations with his rich boss, Mr Roland. Here, for example, are Sorrell and Roland talking after the firing of an arrogant and bullying head porter at the hotel of which Roland is the owner and Sorrell at that time the under-porter.

' "You don't know what a relief this is," said Roland. "How I loathe that class – in the mass. We are outside the pale to them. Their sense of humour – such as it is – does not include us. It wasn't always so.

We are fair game to most of them, we who have anything, or can do anything a little better than the crowd. We are to be robbed, lied to, blackmailed, slandered. Isn't that so?"

"I suppose it is. But – not all – "

"Oh – I know. Some of us have the remnants of souls. I have good people here; I know it. They don't look on me as their natural enemy. To me it is the individual that matters. Breed. Oh, well, what is it? A fastidiousness, a sense of humour and a sense of proportion, the knowledge that hitting a better man than yourself with a pick-handle doesn't make progress. Duty. Wisdom. Disdain and pity instead of scorn. You know." '

Sorrell, a wounded ex-officer with the M.C., is seen as representative of that large body of ex-officers who returned from the War to find themselves either unemployed, or at best unable to find employment in the kind of job which their education and their middle-class upbringing had accustomed them to expect and be able to perform. Sorrell's situation is complicated, dramatized, and only slightly particularized (in the sense that not everyone had precisely these problems), by the fact that he is separated from his wife and has custody of their son. Disgustedly but toughly facing the situation, he dedicates himself and his energies to securing any kind of job that will enable him to support the boy, educate him, and ultimately secure for him the kind of position which Sorrell feels is due to his class and culture. It is to this end that he takes a job as under-porter at an hotel.

He endures many humiliations and bears many burdens, including the menacing sexual voracity of the proprietress. Fortunately his qualities draw him to the attention of Mr Roland, who is not only a successful real estate operator, but also a writer of equally successful musical comedies. Through Roland's good offices and his own abilities, Sorrell becomes, first, head porter, and later Manager of one of Roland's hotels. As head porter, he has a man named Hulks under him. This Hulks is an example of the better type of working man.

'Bert Hulks was proud of his strength and was ready to spend it with healthy enthusiasm, for no one had persuaded him he ought to bottle it up and dole it out in careful drops. He admired Sorrell, and they got on famously.

"Oh yes – I've got a back, but he's got a head, some head."

9
E. M. Hull
*Transworld
Syndication*

10
P. C. Wren
John Murray Limited

11
W. J. Locke
Radio Times Hulton Picture Library

Had any interfering "friend of the people" challenged Bert's attitude towards Sorrell and their work, he might have looked puzzled.

"Being exploited – am I? Don't see it, chum. I've got the back and he's got the head. Besides – he got a bit smashed up in the War. Dicky inside, see. Carrying baggage upstairs doesn't hurt me. He's got the headpiece. We get on champion. What's wrong with that?"

The plain fellow's good nature had solved the problem.'

Because of Sorrell's efficiency, the tips flow in well.

'Sorrell found his poetry in figures. He was enjoying the romance of hard cash. These glittering sixpences, shillings, florins and half-crowns, they were the stars above his immediate world, and of far more significance and import than the stars. His means to an end, his material plunder for immaterial needs. For with his savings he was going to arm his son against a world that babbled of socialism but still clutched a knife or a club.

Skill and knowledge were to be Kit's "arms", some craft in which he could use hand and brain and could say to the miner "Bring coal, or my skill is not for you", or to the baker, "Bread or you die". For Sorrell's sufferings and struggles had not led him towards the illusion of socialism. He had seen too much of human nature. Labour, becoming sectionalized, would split into groups, and group would grab from group, massing for the struggle instead of fighting a lone fight. Only the indispensable and individual few would be able to rise above the scramble of the industrial masses. It is the few who matter and who will always matter. So Sorrell thought.

Social services? Oh, yes, ten thousand years hence – perhaps. But for the moment – arms – and not too much trust in your neighbour.'

Before Sorrell ultimately dies of cancer, he has reached a position of comparative affluence, and his son Kit has attained his ambition of becoming a successful surgeon.

As documentary evidence of particular attitudes to life and society, the views expressed on education are of unusual signifi-

5—B * *

cance. Mr Roland, discussing the future education of Kit with Sorrell, remarks :

' "Education; damned rot – most of it. The healthy young idlers often do best in the end. They don't get all their individuality compressed into a mould. If I had a boy –

I'd let my boy play hard ! I'd have him taught boxing; I wouldn't have him crammed. Natural growth. Later I should give him the best tutor who was to be had."

"And what about his career ?"

"Leave it to his natural appetite. In a clean straight boy who has been treated healthily, the appetite is bound to develop. Surely? And let him go ahead. Tell him to go ahead like blazes." '

Sorrell has secured the services of a Mr Porteous, an able, scholarly, and athletic curate, as private tutor for his son. He later decides to send Christopher to 'one of the best of the private schools'. When Christopher was fourteen, 'Mr Porteous had given him so solid a grounding that he could have held his own with any boy of sixteen.' Sorrell and Mr Porteous discuss the problem of how to find a school in which he, Christopher, will not be exposed to class hatred. For it is not 'a mere question of education but a problem of class prejudices and of social "atmosphere" '.

'As Sorrell put it to Porteous – "Envy – not love – is becoming more and more the driving force. That's how I view it. One now has to weigh up hatreds and prejudices."

Porteous was not wholly in favour of the school.

"What's it going to give him ?"

"Experience – of a sort. Confidence. He will mix with boys of the class that is going to be his, and yet I don't want him to belong to any particular class."

"Can you help it ?"

"I know what you mean. Our voices, our faces, our very way of wearing our clothes put us in a certain category. Because I have set out to give my boy advantages – I shall expose him to hatred and envy."

"My dear chap !"

"Isn't it true? The world has entered on a period of envy

and bitterness. Industrialism and education – of a sort – have
bred it."

"So you think of sending him to school – "

"Where he will not be exposed to class hatred. My idea is
to keep him there two years. Then he can come back to you
for another year or so before he tackles the real adventure."

"Doctoring?"

"That seems to hold."

"A University first?"

"I don't know – yet."

"That will expose him to the sneers of the new young working-class intellectuals."

"I think that he will be exposed to that in any event. As I
see it, the social war is going to grow more and more bitter.
You will be damned by the crowd class even for having a certain sort of voice and face."

"Rather a gloomy view – !"

"No, not gloomy but a little grim. Life is bound to sort
people out, and the envious fool will always end up as the
underdog. I don't mean my boy to be an underdog."

Yet the incident that finally decided both father and son in
the choice of the path that Christopher was to follow was a
trivial one, and yet to Sorrell convincingly significant.

The incident occurred at a boy's football match in which
Mr Porteous' boys' club was playing the Winstonbury Council
School. Kit was playing for the boy's club and Sorrell was
watching the game. He had a knot of noisy youngsters near
him who began to jeer at one particular player.

They called him "Collars and Cuffs". They mocked him
every time he came near them or when he had the ball . . .

What was more, Sorrell saw that the boys of the Council
School team had Christopher marked. They made a dead set
at him; he was something alien; he did not belong to their
class pack. He was different.

Sorrell saw his son "fouled" on more than one occasion and
the boys near him gloated and laughed, but when Kit showed
legitimate spirit in a charge or a tackle, they snarled at him.

"Foul!" "Dirty!"

"Play the game!"

Sorrell walked back with his son after the game and a few
pregnant confidences passed between them.

"Do you like playing with those boys, Kit?" "No, I don't,
pater."

"All right, we'll alter that."

For Sorrell had seen that these sons of working men hated
the son of the ex-officer. They hated his face, his voice, his
pride, his very good temper. They hated him for his differences,
his innocent superiorities.

A hatred, a cheaply educated hatred, was loose in the
world.'

Christopher gets to the school but after a time is asked to
leave, it being discovered that his father is nothing but a hotel
porter.

Sorrell shares with a good many of his fictional contemporaries a profoundly suspicious attitude towards women. Admittedly one may in the end come across a woman who will turn
up trumps. But one is apt to wait a long time and may easily be
disappointed. It seems safest to regard Woman as at the best a
negative, impeding force, and at the worst a dangerous and even
dirty animal. Christopher does find a worth-while girl in the end,
though she nearly eludes him. Earlier, discussing life while punt-
ing on the river at Cambridge, Christopher suddenly remarks,
'What do people want?'

'Sorrell surveyed the first stars.

"That is youth's trouble. It does not know what it wants."

"Didn't you, pater?"

"Vague flashes. No – not clearly. When I look back now I
see that I was in a sort of enchanted fog. You would rush
about and see – sudden things when the fog lifted for a
moment. A bit of red sky, or a tree, or a silly full moon, or a
girl's face. And you thought you wanted the moon or the
girl's face. Perhaps you got one of them – and then the fog
came down again, and you went on groping. But it's worse for
two to be groping."

"It's sex," said Kit suddenly, leaning over his paddle, "sex –
that's what it is."

Sorrell raised himself on one elbow.

"The fog of sex. You have found that out – ! It took me
twenty years, my son. But hush – !"

He laughed.

"We shall shock the May Flies."

Kit surprised him. "They take a lot more shocking than one thinks, pater. We aren't easily shocked. Were you?"

"We pretended to be."

"Why – " He dug the paddle into the water and closed his mouth on some impulsive confession. Sorrell wondered. He told himself that a man got out of date. The young things had different ways of arranging the world, and at present they walked instead of dancing, and eschewed elemental curves. Obviously Kit had met other young things and had parleyed with them. Sorrell's feeling was that for Kit woman was not upon a pedestal.

"You were always saying, pater, that the job matters – more than – other things."

"So it does."

"That's what I think. Sometimes – a chap – feels he must go head over heels into – life."

"Of course," said Sorrell. "The unknown, woman, all that. The thing is – though one does not realise it when one is young, that one wants – the sensation – not the particular woman. One wants all women that ever were. The sensation is natural – but marriage – "

He paused, looking beyond Kit at the grey arch of the bridge.

"Marriage is – artificial. That's the whole trouble. So – you see – "

"You don't believe in marriage --?"

Sorrell would like to have shrugged his shoulders.

"No, – not till the job is launched. After that – a comrade – . But the other thing – like one's morning tub. Not a sort of cement pool in a zoo with two bored animals swimming around." '

Suspicious as he is of women in general, Sorrell is naturally particularly alarmed lest his materialistic, grossly sensual, and highly possessive ex-wife may get her hooks into Christopher. A good deal of the drama revolves around Christopher's relations with his mother. Fortunately for Sorrell, Christopher sees his mother clearly for what she is and is frankly repelled by her. Among many other grounds for satisfaction, Sorrell is able to note that 'As for the so-called "Oedipus Complex", it did not appear to exist in Kit. Nor had it existed in Sorrell. And yet it did not seem to him that either he or his son were abnormal. He rather thought that the abnormality could be looked for on the Continent, and in the mental make-up of a certain sort of Continental youth who grew up to be a professor.'

This view of the Continent in general, and Freud in particular, may be regarded as a clue or key to the general tone and philosophy of *Sorrell and Son*. They were obviously a tone and a philosophy which found a welcome in the hearts of numberless British readers.

When *Sorrell and Son* was first published, it appeared to be, and indeed was, an exceedingly topical book. There were thousands of men in the country in conditions very similar to Sorrell's. Some of them led a miserable and savagely exploited existence, selling vacuum cleaners and other household appliances from door to door. Others invested their gratuities in enterprises, such as chicken-farming, which were for the most part foredoomed for lack of adequate capital. And others were reduced to making up small brass bands which paraded the gutters of Oxford Street, Regent Street, and the main streets of other large cities, hoping to earn pennies by their music. They were confined to the gutters because a police regulation insisted that for these men to appear on the pavements would discommode the general public.

This situation was seen at the time as a national scandal. Ex-Officers Associations lobbied Members of Parliament and the question was constantly raised in the House. For a topical novelist, the situation was, to put it crudely, 'a natural'. And it is natural that Warwick Deeping should have seized upon it and dramatized it. What is curious is that long after the situation upon which the book was based had been dissolved, usually in tragedy, the book seemed to lose nothing of its appeal. It is as though in 1946 someone had written a topical novel in which the motivations of the characters arose principally from the human problems produced by rationing. That could have been a bestseller at the time, but it would be surprising if such a book continued to retain its popularity today. Extreme enthusiasts for Deeping's work might claim that the book's continued success results from it being a story so gripping that it transcends the circumstances of its origin. I find this impossible to believe. It is not as gripping a story as all that. Or, to put it another way, many equally or more gripping stories of life in England have been written since. Certainly it is true that if it were not a good story it would have vanished from the bookstalls long ago. But the excellence of the story alone does not fully explain the appeal, and, as I have already said, the story itself is tightly interwoven with the class situation of the period at which it was written.

What seems to emerge is that although the class situation of which Deeping was writing was specifically of his time, of the early 1920s, the plight of Sorrell and his like was only a vivid dramatization of what the middle class felt about its general situation, and – this is the nub of it – has gone on feeling right up to our own day.

It is one thing for people to claim that the middle class hates, resents, and fears the working class, that it dreams of an elitist society in which, by virtue of its superior education and general culture, it will assume the dominant position which it regards as its due, and that it regards socialism not only as economic and political nonsense but as morally a dirty word. It is quite another thing to possess a document in which these views are vigorously expressed and have been welcomed with hard cash by innumerable readers. In pointing his finger at the menace of the rising working class, Warwick Deeping was carrying out on the home front a task roughly analogous to that performed by Erskine Childers when, in *The Riddle of the Sands*, he pointed to the gathering menace beyond the North Sea.

There was not, to my knowledge, any book published before the First World War which paralleled Childers' warning as to what was happening on the international front by similar warnings directed to the internal situation, the home front. Reading the popular, as distinct from the 'serious', novels of the period, one could suppose that while most people were prepared to believe at least in the possibility of international war, they were blind, despite all the evidence noisily piling up on the industrial scene, to the equally probable imminence of openly violent war. Newspaper headlines reported the evidence almost every day. But the popular novelists were notably coy.

There was at least one good reason for this attitude. An integral part of the moral defences of the middle class consisted precisely in the denial that a class war was in progress at all. In the same way, the phrase 'capitalist system' was generally taboo, for to admit the existence of one system was to admit the possibility of others. It was dangerous to admit or even suggest that there might be some alternative to the capitalist system other than in a fanciful Utopia which nobody was expected to take seriously. The capitalist system was to be regarded as Life, period. As though in compensation for this inhibition, popular novels dealing ostensibly with other themes were fairly freely peppered with references to ill-conditioned agitators, grossly inefficient or more or less humorously nonsensical workers, and hypothetical anarchist plots. For reasons which are obscure – obscure at least to me – these references are most frequent in the thrillers of the period. John Buchan's *The Power House* had as its villain a multi-millionaire anarchist (close relative of Schuabe in *When It Was Dark*), an intimate of Cabinet Ministers, wielding immense secret international power, and so coldly cerebral that if you looked at him when he was off his guard you had the impression that you were looking into the eyes of a snake. (Shuabe's eyes were, it will be remembered, similar in quality.) The fact that snakes are of sub-normal intelligence was no matter to the writer. Ever since the Garden of Eden and probably before that, the serpent had been cunning. Buchan's villain is named Lumley. Significantly he has as his willing tool a shifty-looking fellow who got his training and start in life as a trade-union official. He had stolen the union funds and been expelled, but because of what Buchan considers foolish Radical laws designed to protect the status of trade unions, he could not be prosecuted. His character and career, however, might serve as a warning to militant trade-unionist rank and file. Equally significantly, the hero of *The Power House*, a Tory M.P., has as his loyal ally in the struggle against Lumley a rugged Yorkshire Labour M.P. who, though he makes foolish Radical speeches in the House, has a heart of gold and is happy to account the Tory his best friend. An even more slippery character is held up for our admiration in a subsequent book of Buchan's, *The Three Hostages*. He is ostensibly an Indian Nationalist. In reality, he is a *provocateur* and informer in the pay of the British Government.

I have said that in the popular novels of the period before 1914 references to class conflict were sparse. This is so. On the other hand, A.S.M. Hutchinson, looking back a few years from the early 1920s, evidently remembers vividly the continuous and violent personal controversies which raged among the class of people to whom the pre-war bestsellers were appealing. There is no reason to suppose Hutchinson's memory at fault : everyone who was old enough to listen at that time knows that it is not. Which makes the comparative silence of the bestsellers the more interesting.

In *If Winter Comes*, the hero, Mark Sabre, is shown as shocked and deeply puzzled by the class situation. His attitude is very different from that of Sorrell. And it would appear from the success of the two books that the middle-class book-buying and book-borrowing public of the early 1920s found it as easy to sympathize or identify with Sabre as with Sorrell. 1913, Hutchinson writes, was

'a year of violent feelings violently expressed; and amidst them and because of them, Sabre found with new certainty that he had no violent feelings. Increasingly he came to know that he had well expressed his constitutional habit, the outstanding trait in his character, when on the day of that talk in the office with Nona he had spoken of his disastrous inability – disastrous from the point of view of being satisfactory to single-minded persons or of pulling out that big booming stuff called success – to pursue a thing whatever it might be from a single point of view and go all out for it from that point of view. "Convictions", he had said and often in the welter of antago-nistic convictions of 1913 thought again, "Convictions. If you are going to pull out this big booming stuff they call success, if you are going to be satisfactory to anybody or to anything, you must shut down on everything from everybody's point of view but your own. You must have convictions. And narrower than that – not only convictions but conviction. Conviction that your side is the right side and that the other side is wrong, wrong to blazes.

But he had no such conviction. Above all, and most em-phatically, he had never the conviction that his side whichever side it might be in any of the issues daily tabled for men's dis-cussion was the right side and the other side was the wrong and wicked and disastrous side. In an hour of violent opinions he was by their very violence swayed away from them, their ground washed away from under his feet. He was by tradition

and upbringing and natural inclination a supporter of the
Upper Classes – or, as he preferred to call them, the better-
educated Classes – but five minutes in the company of his Class
engaged in cursing the Liberal Government and all their
works, and the Trade Unionists and all their conspiracies,
threw him angrily and clumsily (his habitual weakness of
expression) into defence of the unspeakable tribes.

"Man, you're nothing better than a Socialist," he was told
in the course of a tirade at the Golf Club.

"I am merely saying," he would reply "you can't help
seeing their point of view. You can't pretend their chances are
equal. You can say it's devilish hard, impossible if you like, to
level up the bricklayer's boy's start in life with the Baronet's
boy's start in life and impossible to level up pay for a day's
work with a spade to a day's work in a profession. You can say
that. But I'm damned if you can say it's all equal or deny that
the underdog does naturally sometimes think it's unfair. I'm
damned if you can say that."

And the other. "Well I damned well can." '

The very next morning we find Sabre in furious argument
against the Radical near-socialist partner, Twyning. Sabre confronted with this near-socialist notes that 'Violence, venom,
hatred was in Twyning's voice and appeared in spittle at the
corners of his mouth; and the venom disgusted Sabre, and the
horrible spittle disgusted him and made him loathe the class of
mind that had such venom and such habits.'

At the end of the argument Twyning says,

' "But I'll tell you this! Things aren't going on like this
much longer. There's going to be equal distribution and equal
opportunity or the people will know why. England's a Class
country. A Class pleasure ground. Well comrade, it's going
to be a masses' country."

"Well, God help it," Sabre said heatedly and turned to his
desk. Driven by what he considered these maddening fallacies
so strongly into the opposite camp as at the Golf Club, he had
been driven out of it by its own rotten worthless arguments.'

'Ahmed! Monseigneur!'

WHEN A WASHINGTON girl, in a famous case, charged a man with rape, the Judge asked her, 'When did this rape occur?' 'When did it occur?' she cried. 'Why, Judge, it was rape, rape, rape all summer long.' The statement succinctly describes the theme of E. M. Hull's *The Sheik*. Week after week after week of fierce rape amid sights and scenes of Araby while Saharan stars shone mysteriously down. The public was flat on its back gasping for more in five languages, and Rudolf Valentino was provided with his most famous role.

Sado-masochism, prettily packaged, and selling well as usual? Something of that, no doubt; quite a lot. How that beautiful white girl, almost whiter than white, squirms and struggles in those steely Sheikish arms until 'her whole body was one agonized ache from the brutal hands that enforced her to compliance, until her courageous spirit was crushed by . . . the strange fear that the man himself awakened in her, which had driven her at last moaning to her knees!' Kidnapped by this Sheik, and, to her continuing horror, raped almost every night, the high-born English girl finds the days alarming, too. At one moment the Sheik beats a servant half to death. 'She had watched, fascinated with horror, until he had tossed away the murderous whip, and without a second glance at the limp, blood-stained heap that huddled on the ground with suggestive stillness had strolled back unconcerned to the tent . . . She hated him with all the strength of her proud passionate nature.' Next time out, the Sheik breaks a wild colt in 'a hideous exhibition of brute strength and merciless cruelty. Diana was almost sick with horror from the beginning; she longed to turn away, but her eyes clung fascinated.'

The episode is intended as a sharp lesson to 'proud Diana Mayo, who had the history of her race at her fingers' ends, and

had gloried in the long line of upright men and chaste women.'
Says the Sheik,

 ' "Would it not be wiser, after what you have seen today, to
recognize that I am master?"
 "You mean that you will treat me as you treated the colt
this afternoon?" she whispered . . .
 "I mean that you must realize that my will is law."
 "And if I do not?"
 "Then I will teach you, and I think that you will learn –
soon."
 She quivered in his hands.'

Contemporaries agree that a lot of people did regard *The
Sheik* as basically pornographic, a tease-act not redeemed by the
ultimate burgeoning of one-hundred-per-cent love in the oasis.

 They were, so far as may be judged at this distance, less vocal
in protest than current protesters against sex and violence on TV.
But they did spread the word (a) that *The Sheik* was unsuitable
reading for young people on account of the fact that it not only
went on and on about rape, but showed rape ultimately rewar-
ded; and (b) that it was 'trashy', and was – so this sort of critics
said – 'read only by under-housemaids'. This second barrel of
criticism was evidently intended to pepper those who might not
have been scared off by the accusation of sexually immoral tendencies.

 The sales went booming on. And not by any means only
among the 'under-housemaids' – or whatever subsection of
society and somewhat anachronistic phrase may have been intended to point disdainfully at. Diana Mayo's experiences, as
reported by E. M. Hull, were after all worth putting on the
agenda of intimate talks at the bridge clubs. What, quite frankly,
and strictly between ourselves, it might be asked, was Mrs Peri-
winkle's feeling about a situation in which a girl is raped and
raped, hates every minute of raw sexual intercourse with this
lusty great brute, and suddenly at the end of two or three
months finds she loves him madly?

 This tremendous emotional turnabout occurs with maximum
melodramatic impact. She flees from the Sheik. He pursues her.
She is riding the grey, Silver Star, he the black Hawk.
Faster and faster they dash across the desert. 'Would it not be

possible for Silver Star, carrying the lighter burden, to out-
distance The Hawk? It was a chance. She would take it, but she
would never give in. The perspiration was rolling down her face
and her breath was coming laboriously.'

The Sheik shouts to her that he will shoot her horse. 'She
would not stop; nothing on earth should make her stop now.
Only, because she knew the man, she kicked her feet clear of the
stirrups. He had said he would shoot, and he would shoot, and
if the grey shied or swerved a hair's breadth she would probably
receive the bullet that was meant for him. Better that! Yes, even
better that!'

He shoots. Silver Star drops. The Sheik brings The Hawk to
where she is lying, 'tossed her up roughly into the saddle and
swung up behind her, the black breaking at once into the usual
headlong gallop'.

Presently she is 'lying across the saddle in front of the Sheik,
and he was holding her in the crook of his arm'. The Hawk
gallops on through the night. And it is in this posture and under
these circumstances that revulsion turns suddenly to love.

'With a start of recollection she realized fully whose arm was
around her, and whose breast her head was resting on. Her
heart beat with sudden violence. What was the matter with
her? Why did she not shrink from the pressure of his arm and
the contact of his warm, strong body? What had happened
to her? Quite suddenly she knew – knew that she loved him,
that she had loved him for a long time, even when she thought
she hated him and when she had fled from him ... Love had
come to her at last who had scorned it so fiercely. The men
who had loved her [these were well-born Englishmen] had
not had the power to touch her, she had given love to no one,
she had thought that she could not love, that she was devoid
of all natural affection and that she would never know what
love meant. But she knew now – a love of such complete sur-
render as she had never conceived. Her heart was given for all
time to the fierce desert man who was so different from all
other men she had met, a lawless savage who had taken her to
satisfy a passing fancy and who had treated her with merciless
cruelty. He was a brute, but she loved him, loved him for his
very brutality, and superb animal strength. And he was an
Arab! A man of different race and colour, a native; Aubrey

[her brother] would indiscriminately class him as "a damned nigger". She did not care. A year ago, a few weeks even, she would have shuddered with repulsion at the bare idea, the thought that a native could even touch her had been revolting, but all that was swept away and was as nothing in the face of the love that filled her heart so completely . . . She was deliriously, insanely happy.'

Diana's big moment under the stars was unquestionably a big moment too for many thousands of women who felt, as they read, that they would give much to exchange their sofas for the bounding back of The Hawk, with the warm strong body of the Sheik pressing from behind. Unerringly, the author had secured a horde of sex-starved women for her readership. (She had already provided their imaginations with a physically detailed picture of the Sheik such as could be almost effortlessly evoked even on a wet day in England.)

It is always, as the historian and sociologist well know, difficult to determine just who 'started something' and when. But there is a great deal to be said for the view that it was that night-ride on The Hawk which 'started' among innumerable English women, well-born or not, the practice of taking when possible a holiday in North Africa, in the hope that where *the* Sheik had been, other Sheiks might be.

There are travel agents, even today, who believe that a high percentage of women clients, cruising alone to the southern Mediterranean, have actually read *The Sheik* and booked their passage on the strength of it. Others more cautiously admit that in their view it is certainly the 'Sheik mystique' invented by E. M. Hull which induces these pilgrims to choose this particular outing, even if they have not themselves read the book.

But though that ride and its consequences were the main motive force which sent *The Sheik* marching through the book-stalls of Britain, Europe, and the United States, the book had other attractions. It is not to be supposed that the appeal to the public of the 1920s would have been so great, even in E. M. Hull's skilled presentation, had the *mise-en-scène* been a villa on the South Downs, Miss Mayo the kidnapped daughter of a Brighton bank manager, and the Sheik an Algerian student reading Agriculture and Forestry at Oxford. The desert, the escape, the assurance of being 'away from it all' is essential.

Pacific island beaches were getting crowded, and for purposes of escape a dream-Sahara was just as nice as a blue lagoon. In the 1970s there is not much unspoiled dream-country left. Trippers everywhere, or else politics. Get away for a bit of romance on the sun-kissed sands of magical Ceylon, and next thing you know they are asking are you a Maoist or a neo-Trotskyist? The simpler sort of science-fiction provides a solution to this problem of overcrowding at the escape resorts. But in the 1920s the Sahara was barely touched by the hand of the developer.

The high class level of the principals was of evident importance. Snobbery is always with us, and there is no valid reason for sneering at Miss Mayo's ancestry. But, having established her encampment on this high plateau, authoress Hull faced a tricky problem. That a dark-hued, damn nearly black, Arab should kidnap and wreak his will on an aristocratic English girl very keen on blood sports is to be expected. But how is it going to look if she falls in love with him? Insists on living with the blackish fellow ever after? But naturally things are not what, until page 190 or thereabouts, they seem. A French friend of the Sheik, and a reliable informant since he is not only a Vicomte but one of the old, as distinct from the new, *noblesse*, discloses to Diana the glorious truth – a truth which explains incidentally why he, to her earlier puzzlement, has always taken such trouble to keep his finger-nails clean.

Her passionately beloved Sheik is not an Arab at all. He is the son of a tip-top British peer and his beautiful Spanish wife who is the scion of one of the oldest noble families in Spain – so old and so noble that it is quite all right to hint that they may have had Moorish blood from way back. This same peer was, at the time of his wedding to the teen-aged Spanish beauty, an alcoholic, and when drunk he had fits of ungovernable temper and behaved in an unmentionable manner. One day, on a trip to Algiers, he hit the bottle badly, and behaved worse, if possible, than ever before. Horrified, and pregnant to boot, the girl escaped and ran out into the desert.

There she was found wandering by a genuinely Arabian, but still very fine, very rich, very powerful, Sheik. Welcomed, protected, and platonically loved by this Sheik, she gave birth to a boy and in due course died, refusing to disclose the story of her life. But she left a sealed document explaining it all, which was to be made known to the son when he grew up. Under the influence of the old Vicomte, the lad was educated partly in France, partly in England.

Informed at last of the facts, he curses his father prolongedly in two languages for his ill-treatment of his mother, vows eternal hatred of all things English, and, shaking off the corrupt dust of Europe, goes back to the pure, exhilarating air of the desert. He succeeds to the power and position of the old Sheik (whose son he is generally thought to be) and goes on the waggon for life. (He is not, however, austere to a point where his asceticism might repel the normal reader. He chain-smokes. And we already know a good deal about his sexual behaviour.) Everyone can now see as socially acceptable Miss Mayo's behaviour when, on the last page, she 'slid her arm up behind his neck, drawing his head down. "I am not afraid," she murmured slowly. "I am not afraid of anything with your arms around me, my desert lover. Ahmed! Monseigneur!" ' Everything is race-wise and class-wise O.K.

O.K., too, were the basic gimmicks, if one may so describe them, of another gloriously successful literary foray into the Sahara conducted a couple of years later under the leadership of P. C. Wren, author of *Beau Geste*, a book welcomed by, for instance, the *Daily Telegraph* as 'a story of rare quality from every point of view. It stirs the blood, holds fast the interest, and kindles the imagination'. You could say that again. You could, indeed, say it fifty-one times, which was the number of editions the book had gone into by the fortieth anniversary of its first publication in the year 1924. With Wren we not only spend many pages under the pitiless Saharan sun, we do so inside the famed Foreign Legion. As his publishers state on the blurb of the forty-ninth edition, 'Wren had, of course, an advantage over most of his imitators. He had been a Legionnaire himself, and wrote of what he knew.' This was true. It is fair to say, too, that E. M. Hull had blazed quite a trail across those burning sands.

It is much to the credit of Wren's acumen and understanding of English taste that he realized how soggily a merely realistic novel with a Foreign Legion background could flop. The Foreign Legion picture had to be suitably framed; flamboyantly framed. And frame it he did in a plot which, if not exactly neat, was certainly gaudy.

His plot was, when you come right down to it, grotesque. So

for the matter of that was the plot of *The Sheik*. Anyone who tries to fault either of these books on that ground has a poor understanding of what literature, as a branch of show-business, is about. (Just take a line through that world bestseller *The Count of Monte Cristo*.) To be preposterous, to cock snooks at the normally credible, to suspend, however briefly, unbelief, to take the reader on a trip to the wide blue yonder, to get one more flight out of an imaginary but ever so noble aristocracy while indicating one's modern awareness that the old bus might be conking out – these are notable achievements, notably achieved by a whole sales-force of authors.

The opening of *Beau Geste* is superb: we have a French fort in the desert where the force coming to relieve the garrison finds everyone inside it dead, but propped up behind the loo holes and the sandbags, with their rifles, in lifeless hands, trained on an invisible enemy. It is splendidly done. How come? You may well ask, but it would take a whole book to explain the situation in detail, and if anyone really wants an answer to the question he can certainly still get *Beau Geste* at the library.

But why 'Beau Geste'? Who is 'Beau Geste'? Well, not putting too fine a point on it, he's a sort of pun. That is to say, the name of his aristocratic family is Geste. Then 'by reason of his remarkable physical beauty, mental brilliance and general distinction' Michael Geste is dubbed by one and all 'beau' Geste. And then he provides the trigger and the motivation of the whole action of the book by performing an amazingly quixotic and chivalric action : a *beau geste* in fact. A great talking-point in itself. ('Don't you see, darling, he's a "beau" Geste who makes a *beau geste*.' 'Oh I say, that's damned ingenious.')

His aunt and the tenantry on her estate are the intended beneficiaries of Michael's *beau geste*. This aunt is Lady Brandon, who 'had contracted an alliance with Sir Hector Brandon as one might contract a disease.' Hector is a big-game hunter. But he is also utterly selfish, grossly improvident and greedy for money, and a conspicuous lecher. The Brandons have in their possession an enormous, priceless sapphire, believed to have been stolen by an earlier Sir Hector from 'the Sultan of Mysore' and known as the 'Blue Water'.

Recking of naught but his own disreputable pleasures, the present Sir Hector keeps spending the money essential for the upkeep of the estate and the physical welfare of the dependent tenants. The good Lady Brandon secretly sells the Blue Water to an agent of the ruling Maharajah of Mysore to raise money for the tenantry. She has a cheap substitute made, but is driven to panic by sudden news that Sir Hector is unexpectedly returning from his travels, and will certainly discover the deception.

To save her, Michael steals the substitute, so that his aunt can tell Sir Hector the Blue Water has been burgled. Unfortunately, Lady Brandon refuses to believe that the burglary is an outside job, and suspicion falls on various innocent young relatives living in her house. In order to prove to police and, ultimately, Sir Hector that the stone really has been stolen, and to divert attention from the innocent, Michael makes his beautiful gesture. He writes a 'confession', disappears, and joins the Foreign Legion. His twin brother Digby, known as 'Small Geste', struck by the nobility of Michael's action, and feeling he cannot allow him to assume the whole weight of guilt, writes a confession, disappears, and joins the Foreign Legion. Their youngest brother, known naturally as 'Very Small Geste', is deeply moved by their actions. He feels that he, too, must take a share of the supposed guilt. He disappears, gets to Paris, finds the necessary recruiting office, and joins the Foreign Legion.

Naturally enough, they all bump into one another in north Africa, though later separated by the harsh exigencies of the service, and much battle, bloodshed, mystery, and horror. The active service and the bloodshed are admirably described. Within the frame of coincidental absurdities, the author writes with compelling authenticity, and creates situations of tension which fully justify the most extravagant publisher's blurb. They all find their way to that sinister fort where, at the outset of the book, everyone is mysteriously dead.

Michael has been killed in the final battle for the fort. Small Geste and Very Small Geste escape. But before reaching civilization, Small Geste is killed too. Only Very Small Geste survives, to bring to his aunt Michael's last letter, explaining his original action and its motives, and returning the 'clever piece of glass or quartz or whatever it is', the substitute Blue Water.

Michael writes,

' "It nearly made me regret what I had done when those asses Digby and John had the cheek to bolt, too. Honestly, it never occurred to me that they would do anything so silly.

But I suppose it is selfish of me to want all the blame and all the fun and pleasure of doing a little job for you."

"A *beau geste*, indeed," said Aunt Patricia and for the only time in my life I saw her put her handkerchief to her eyes.'

Sir Hector, providentially, has 'died miserably, alone in Kashmir, of cholera – his servants and coolies having fled as soon as the disease was recognised for what it was.'

Aunt Patricia is therefore free to justify nephew Michael's sacrifice for her well-being and happiness by marrying a distinguished member of the Nigerian Civil Service who has loved her from page one onwards.

Reflecting upon the characters of Beau Geste and Sheik Ahmed Ben Hassan Glencaryll, except during the period when hatred and bitterness temporarily soured the latter's lovable and noble qualities, one may properly recall by way of epitaph Albert Chevalier's old music-hall song :

> 'Such a nice man, too,
> Such a very nice man;
> No airs to him, nor beastly affectation.
> One as somehow made yer feel
> As yer reelly had to deal
> With a gentleman, by birth and education.'

The seemingly inexhaustible appeal of *Beau Geste* through all the familiar 'changes in the public taste', despite all the social hell and high water that has swept over the English scene since 1924, is a sufficiently interesting and significant phenomenon. The simple explanation, namely that this proves once again that a 'rattling good yarn' has incalculable powers of survival, is valid so far as it goes. It can even survive a plot of breath-taking, shamelessly audacious, absurdity.

One may, however, speculate as to whether today the central yarn is read *despite* the frame with which it is lumbered. For today's reader is the plot a liability rather than an asset? Or, alternatively, does the modern reader savour the plot as an agreeable bit of period decor? And if so, does a reader of, say, seventeen in 1971 imagine that the decor is historically genuine, representing the sort of thing that actually happened, the sort of way people actually thought in those distant 1920s?

Indeed a further question asks itself: did the mass of the original readers really suppose that somewhere, high in the social empyrean, there were people liable to think and act in this way? Or were they aware that all this had as little relation to historical reality as the fictional behaviour of courtiers and fair ladies in lush 'historical' romances set, say, in the reign of Good Queen Bess?

Vagabond but gentleman too

THE VIEW FROM the shelves of the lending libraries included not only those deep blue lagoons, and the wide stretches of the Sahara, but also the Sea Coast of Bohemia. The prospect offered was varied indeed, and it would seem that the beaches of that shore catered for almost every type of tourist. Shifts in the meaning of words as a means of gauging the changing attitudes of those who use them are a well known and valuable subject of study. 'Bohemian' is a word worth attention. Leaving behind the period when it meant simply a gipsy, it became a chameleon. It meant different things, not only at different times but often to different people at the same time. It could be used in a totally pejorative sense, indicating that the writer or speaker considered the 'Bohemian' a dissolute vagabond, immoral and dishonest, and possessing all the qualities which one would not wish to find in a man about to marry one's sister. At other times or to other people it suggested the picture of a person or a family who might be outsiders as far as properly established and well-conducted members of the community were concerned, but at the same time could be decent, jolly, amusing, and even – in their peculiar way – have certain insights, into the problems and perplexities of humanity. From there the Bohemian could go on at a later date to develop into an enviable being, free of the tiresome restrictions which hemmed in more conventional people, but still a little dangerous, or even very dangerous, precisely on this very account. The helpless Bohemian could also be brigaded at will as a kind of cultural bank-robber engaged by the author to attack the intellectual strong-rooms of the bourgeoisie.

Although always, and by definition, an outsider, on the whole his character improved throughout the latter part of the nineteenth century. Even so, we may recall the alarmed reaction of the vicar's daughter in *When It Was Dark* to the news that her

fiancé, the curate, was about to share chambers in London with
two bachelor friends. She was reassured by her father. 'The
days when you couldn't be a genius without being dirty are
gone,' said the vicar. 'I am glad of it. I was staying at St Ives
last summer, where there is quite an artistic settlement. All the
painters carried golf clubs and looked like professional athletes.'
Here the vicar made a joke. He said, 'They drink Bohea in
Bohemia now.'

Even at that date, not everyone wanted artists to look like
professional athletes and spend their time on the golf links.
They enjoyed a literary walk out with a gay, unconventional,
free, even irreverent type of Bohemian and in 1906 their needs
were amply satisfied by *The Beloved Vagabond*, a novel by W.
J. Locke. The blurb to the latest edition of this immensely popular work presents the ingredients of appeal in a few succinct lines :

> '*The Beloved Vagabond* is an irresistible story of the open
> road and the free life. The hero is a "wandering philosopher"
> who rescues a small boy from poverty, adopts him and takes
> him on his wanderings through Europe, educating him on the
> way.
> This is a happy story of a ne'er-do-well whose fascinating
> life and adventures on the roads of Europe make us realise
> how attractive the unconventional life can be.'

No harm in describing the plot as preposterous; preposterous
is clearly what it was intended to be. It is as visibly 'contrived'
as a musical box, and as predictable. This is not to say that the
contrivance cannot repeatedly and almost continuously produce
deeper notes evoking thoughts about the meaning of life, civilization, society, and the nature of love. The central figure is as
well-equipped a Bohemian as ever played the role. He is the
son of a French father and an Irish mother, a parentage which
is automatically seen to explain, and where necessary excuse,
his finest qualities and his defects. Indeed, he is not just French
on his father's side, but Gascon to boot. His real name is Gaston
de Nérac. But for the greater part of the book he roams freely,
philosophizes, plays the violin for a living (a wandering minstrel
he), and drinks a great deal of absinthe under the name of
Berzelius Nibbidard Paragot.

The narrator is at the outset a small Cockney boy named

Augustus Smith. Adopting him as his boy-of-all-work and pupil, Paragot changes the lad's name to Asticot. Early in their relationship, in Paragot's disreputable rooms in Tavistock Street, Asticot finds some papers stuffed into an old stocking. Reading them, he discovers a good deal about his master's past and his views. Evidently he was at one time in love with a beautiful lady named Joanna: *'pure et ravissante comme une aube d'Avril.'* Other notes scribbled by Paragot at one time and another help swiftly to draw his picture.

'At Prague I made the aquaintance of a polite burglar who introduced me to his lady wife and to other courteous criminals, their spouses and families . . . Granted their sociological premises, based on Proudhon, they are too logical. The lack of imaginative power to break away from convention, *their convention*, is a serious defect in their character. They take their gospel of *tuum est meum* too seriously. I do not inordinately sympathise with people who get themselves hanged for a principle.'

Encouraging! In the same paragraph it is suggested that disciples of Proudhon are likely to be criminals and the reader is assured that he is not going to be asked to admire some seriously political subversive. The narrator notes:

'I also see now, as of course I could not be expected to see then, that Paragot, being a creature of extremes, would either have the highest or lowest. In these troubled sketches, as he cannot go to Grand Hotels, I find him avoiding like lazar-houses the commercial or family hostelries, where he will foregather with the half-educated, the half-bred, the half-souled; the offence of them is too rank for his spirit. The pretending simian class, aping the vices of the rich and instinct with the vices of the low, and frank in neither, moves the man's furious scorn. He will have realities at any cost. All said and done, the bugs of Novortovshakaya did not masquerade as humming-birds, nor merry Giuseppi Sacconi of Verona as a critic of Girolami dai Libri.'

Paragot is manager of a satisfactorily Bohemian club called the Lotus.

'During the daytime it was an abode of abominable desolation. No one came near it till nine o'clock in the evening, when one or two members straggled in, took down their long pipes and called for whisky or beer, the only alcoholic beverages the club provided . . . At eleven the cloth was laid. From then till half past members came in considerable numbers. At half past supper was served. A steaming dish of tripe furnished the head of the table in front of Paragot and a cut of cold beef the foot.

There were generally from fifteen to thirty present; men of all classes: journalists, actors, lawyers, out-at-elbows nondescripts. I have seen one of Her Majesty's judges and a prizefighter exchanging views across the table. They supped, talked, smoked and drank whisky up to two or three o'clock in the morning, and appeared to enjoy themselves prodigiously.'

Losing his job as manager of the Lotus, and smashing a violin over the head of the mean-souled owner, Paragot takes off for France. He and Asticot wander for a year through Europe. Then, the following spring, they arrive in Savoy. Outside a village they encounter a peasant girl and an elderly man who are on their way to Chambéry, to play the zither and the violin at a wedding. Almost immediately, the old man dies of exhaustion. Paragot appoints himself his successor, takes the girl Blanquette under his wing, and the three wander on to Aix-les-Bains.

'Not being content to having attached to his person the stray dog and a mongrel boy and rendering himself responsible to their destinies, Paragot must now saddle himself with a young woman. Had she been a beautiful gipsy holding fascinating allurements in lustrous eyes and pomegranate lips, and witchery in a supple figure, the act would have been a commonplace of human weakness. But in the case of poor Blanquette, squat and coarse, her heavy features only redeemed from ugliness by youth, honesty and clean teeth, the eternal attraction of sex was absent . . .

Of course he saved the girl from a hideous doom. Thousands of kindly honest men have done the same in one way or another. But Paragot's way was different from anyone else's. Its glorious lunacy lifted it above ordinary human methods

So many of your wildly impulsive people repent them of their generosities as soon as the magnanimous fervour has cooled. The grandeur of Paragot lay in the fact that he never repented. He was fantastic, self-indulgent, wastrel, braggart, what you will; but he had an exaggerated notion of the value of every human soul save his own. The destiny of the poor Blanquette was to him infinitely more important than that of the wayward genius that was Paragot. His point of view had struck me even as a child when he discoursed on my prospects.

"I am Paragot, my son," he would say. "A film full of wind and wonder, fantasy and folly, driven like thistledown above the world. I do not count. But you, my little Asticot, have the Great Responsibility before you. It is for you to uplift a corner of the veil of Life and show joy to men and women where they would not have sought it. Work now and gather wisdom, my son, so that when the Great Day comes you may not miss your destiny." And once he added wistfully – "as I have missed mine".'

And then in the romantic setting of the Restaurant du Lac at Lucerne a romantic thing happens. While Paragot is playing the violin and Asticot is going round with the tambourine used as a collecting box, the beautiful lady out of Paragot's past life is discovered sitting with companions at a table.

This beautiful lady, Joanna, converses with Asticot, cross-questioning him about Paragot's way of life, and finally tells him that she is the Comtesse de Verneuil. She gives him her address in Paris, telling him that if they are ever in trouble and she can help, she will do so.

After this encounter the trio wander on. They reach Budapest. Here Paragot breaks his ankle and also inherits a small patrimony from an aunt. He provides for Asticot to spend the next two years in Budapest, studying art. At the end of that time they are reunited in Paris, where Paragot has established himself as a sort of King Bohemian and super philosopher among the Bohemians of the Café Delphine. Meeting Joanna by accident, Asticot tells her of Paragot's presence in Paris. She seeks him out at the Café Delphine, and begs him to come to see her husband who is ill. He does so. He finds himself in anguished love again after all these thirteen years since he left Joanna for the first time. Then one night she comes to the café to find Paragot. He is drunk, but she and Asticot get him to her house. The Comte de Verneuil, desperately ill in an adjoining room, gives Paragot a document – which he is intended to destroy. But Joanna reads it. She finds it to be a contract, drawn up and signed thirteen years before, by which de Nérac (Paragot) binds himself in consideration of the payment of ten thousand pounds, to leave Joanna's flat and never approach her again.

Joanna is almost speechless with agony at this disclosure of her lover's perfidy. They part again.

This apparently fearful imbroglio is quickly cleared up. The Comte de Verneuil dies, and on his death-bed confesses all to Joanna. It seems that in London thirteen years ago, the Comte de Verneuil had been a crooked financial speculator. Joanna's father, Mr Rushworth, a solicitor in very fashionable practice, was also a company promoter and became the 'tool and dupe, and drawer in general of chestnuts from the fire, for the Comte de Verneuil and his backers'.

Soon the father is in danger not only of bankruptcy but of imprisonment for fraud. On the very night of the party held to celebrate Joanna's engagement to Gaston de Nérac the Comte de Verneuil draws Gaston aside and explains the situation to him.

Ten thousand pounds of his clients' money which Rushworth held in trust had gone in the failure of the company. If that amount was not at his disposal the next morning he was finished, snuffed out. It appeared that no one in Paris or London would lend him the money, his credit being gone. Unless M. de Nérac could find the ten thousand pounds, there was the gaol yawning with horrible certainty for M. de Nérac's prospective father-in-law. As Paragot's patrimony, invested in French Government securities, was not a third of this sum, he could do nothing but wring his hands in despair and call on Providence and the Comte de Verneuil. The former turned a deaf ear. The latter declared himself a man of business and not a philanthropist; he was ready, however, to purchase an option on the young lady's affections. Did not M. de Nérac know what an option was? He would explain. He drafted the famous contract. In return for Paragot's signature he would hand him a cheque drawn in favour of Simon Rushworth.'

Faithful to the terms of the contract, de Nérac disappeared from Joanna's life. The blackguardly de Verneuil first poisoned Joanna's mind against her former fiancé, then told her that he was dead – an acquaintance had found him in a Paris hospital and had paid for his funeral. She believed him. Urged by her parents, she finally accepted to marry de Verneuil. Now, the Comte being dead and Paragot very much alive, the way is open for him to marry Joanna.

At this point there is going to be a question in the reader's mind as to whether Paragot, or even de Nérac, is a suitable husband for a woman who has already been described as 'exquisite', 'fragrant', and 'an English rosebud wet with morning dew'. Fourteen years earlier Gaston de Nérac could have been seen as a suitable man. But think of his subsequent life as Paragot. An associate of riff-raff, a hard-living Bohemian. A person of absolutely no fixed address. Readers who might have been worried about this were immediately reassured. They and the astonished Asticot suddenly learn that all along de Nérac has been a second cousin of Joanna's; he was at school at Rugby, he was a brilliant architect who actually won the *Prix de Rome,* which, as Asticot puts it 'to a Paris art student . . . is what a Field Marshal is to a private soldier, a Lord Chancellor to the eater of dinners in the Temple'. He is at least as acceptable as that Sheik Ahmed.

These insignia of ultimate respectability are the more necessary because Paragot is about to go to stay with Joanna's mother in her old Georgian house at the end of the High Street of Melford in Wiltshire. He is going to meet the County and bits of the hunting set. His strictures upon them are going to be severe, and his behaviour towards them verging on the uncouth. The sight of a genuine, hundred-per-cent-born-and-bred Bohemian relieving himself, spiritually speaking, on the carpets of nice people in Wiltshire might have been a little hard to take for some readers, a little rough. But since the fellow is in reality an Old Rugbeian one can safely and with a sense of cultural superiority take the side of the pseudo-Bohemian against this collection of inhibited snobs.

Locke has made admirable arrangements for his public to have it both ways. Thus, at one of Mrs Rushworth's At Homes, we find Paragot 'talking to an elderly and bony female with a great beak of a nose. I wondered how so unprepossessing a person could be admitted into so fine an assembly and I learned later that she was Lady Molyneux, one of the Great Personages of the county. The lady seemed to be emphatic. So did Paragot. She regarded him stonily out of flint-blue eyes. He waved his hands. She raised her eyebrows. She was one of those women whose eyebrows in the normal state are about three inches from the eyelids. I understood then what super-ciliousness meant. Paragot raised his voice. At that moment one of those strange coincidences occurred in which the ends of all casual conversation fell together, and a shaft of silence spread through the room killing all sound save that of Paragot's utterance.

"But Great Heavens, Madam, babies don't grow in the cabbage-patch, and you are all well aware they don't, and it is criminal of your English writers to mislead the young as to the facts of existence. Charlotte Yonge is infinitely more immoral than Guy de Maupassant."

Then Paragot realised the deadly stillness. He rose from his chair, looked round at the shocked faces of the women, and laughing turned to Mrs Rushworth.

"I was stating Zola to be a great ethical teacher and Lady Molyneux seemed disinclined to believe me."

"He is an author very little read in Melford," said the placid lady from her sofa cushions, whilst the two or three women with whom she was in converse gazed disapprovingly at my master. "It would do the town good if it was steeped in his writings," said he.'

After the party Paragot expounds to Asticot the predictable views of a Bohemian observing the English 'County'.

'My son . . . as a philosopher and a citizen of the world you will find Melford needs a patient study as much as Chambéry or Budapest or the Latin quarter. It is a garden of Lilliput. Here you will see life in its most cultivated littleness. A great passion bursting out across the way will convulse the town like an earthquake. Observe at the same time how constant a factor is human nature. However variable the manifestation may be, the degree is invariable. In spacious conditions it manifests itself in passion, in narrow ones in prejudices. The females in and out of petticoats who were here this afternoon experienced the same thrill in expressing their dislike of me as a person foreign to their conventions, as the Sicilian who plunges his dagger into a rival's bosom. When I marry, my son, I shall not live at Melford . . . I must have room, my son, for development of my genius. I must dream great things, and immortal visions are blasted under the basilisk eye of Lady Molyneux.'

Naturally he has a thing or two to say about a church wedding. 'You must forgive me, *ma chérie*,' he says to Joanna, 'I am a happy Pagan and it is so long since I have met anyone who belonged to the Church of England that I thought the institution had perished of inanition.'

'Why, you went with me to church last Sunday.'

'So I did,' said he, 'but I thought it was only to worship the great British God Respectability.'

Paragot also, of course, falls foul of Major Walters – an Aunt-Sally-type British Military man.

' "He is a man," said Paragot, "in that he is brave and masculine; in that he is intelligent, he is nought. He is a machine-gun. He fires off rounds of stereotype conversation at the rate of one a minute, which is funereal. I have the misfortune, my little Asticot, to be under the ban of Major Walters's displeasure. Your British military man is prejudiced against anyone who is not cut out according to pattern . . . Do you know what he had the impertinence to ask me yesterday? What settlements I proposed to make on Madame de Verneuil. Settlements, mon petit Asticot! He spoke as trustee, whatever that may be, under her husband's will. "Sir," said I, "I will settle my love and my genius upon her, and thereby ensure her happiness and prosperity. Besides, Madame de Verneuil has a fortune which will suffice her needs and of which I will not touch a penny."

I smiled, for I could see Paragot in his grand French manner, one hand thrust between the buttons of his coat, and the other waving magnificently, as he proclaimed himself to Major Walters.

"I explained," he continued, "in terms which I thought

might reach his intelligence, that I only had to resume my profession and my financial position would equal that of Madame Verneuil. And, Sir, said I, I will not suffer you to say another word. We bowed and parted enemies. Wherefore the conversation of the excellent Major Walters does not appeal to me as attractive." '

Before long the suffocating atmosphere of Melford becomes too much for Paragot.

' "It came to a point where I must either expire or go. I decided not to expire. These things are done all in a flash. I was walking in the garden. It was last Sunday afternoon — I remember now : a sodden November day. Imagine a sodden November Sunday afternoon in an English country-town garden. Joanna was at a children's service. Ah, *mon Dieu!* The desolation of that Sunday afternoon! The Death, my son, that was in the air! Ah! I choked, I struggled. The garden wall, the leaden sky closed in upon me, I walked out. I came back to Paris."

"Just like that?" I murmured.

"Just like that," said he. "You may have noticed, my son, that I am a man of swift decisions and prompt action. I walked to the railway station. A providential London train was expected in five minutes. I took it. *Voila!*" '

Paragot has realized that he and Joanna have 'escaped a life-long misery but on the other hand they had lost a lifelong dream . . . The twain had been romantic, walking in the Valley of Illusion, wilfully blinding their eyes to the irony of Things Real. Love had flown far from them during the silent years and they had mistaken the afterglow of his wings for the living radiance. They had begun to realize the desolate truth.'

After a brief period of Bohemian debauchery in Paris, he decides to leave for the country.

' "It is a city of Dead Sea apples. It has no place for me, save the sewer. I don't like the sewer. I am going away. I shall never come back to Paris again."

"But where are you going, master?" I asked, in some surprise.

He did not know. He would pack his bundle and flee like Christian from the accursed city, like Christian he would go on a Pilgrim's Progress. He would seek sweet pure things. He would go forth and work in the field. The old life had come to an end. The sow had been mistaken. It could not return to its wallowing in the mire. Wallowing was disgustful. Was ever man in such a position? The vagabond life had made the conventions of civilization impossible. The contact with convention and clean English ways had killed his zest for the old order of which only the mud remained. There was nothing for it but to leave Paris.'

At this point Asticot suggests to him that he should marry Blanquette, the ill-favoured but loyal girl who has of course been slavishly in love with him all the time. Asticot for his part immediately discovers that Blanquette is the solution to his own woman-problem.

'But it was written, my son, Asticot. It was preordained. She is the one woman in the world to whom I need not pretend to be other than I am. She is real, *mon Dieu!* What she says is Blanquette, what she does is Blanquette and her sayings and doings would grace the greatest Queen in Christendom. But have you thought of it? I have come indeed to the end of my journey. I started out to find Truth, the Reality of Things. I have found it. I have found it, my son. It is a woman, strong and steadfast, who looks into your eyes; who can help a man to accomplish his destiny. And the destiny of man is to work, and to beget strong children. And his reward is to have the light in the wife's eyes and the welcome of a child's voice as he crosses the threshold of his house. And it cleanses a man.'

He marries Blanquette and Joanna marries Major Walters. When Asticot next visits Paragot and Blanquette they are living on a farm and have an eighteen-months-old child. Paragot announces himself totally happy. And he concludes with the words: 'All that the wisdom of all the ages can tell us is summed up in the last words of one of the wisest books that was ever written: "We must cultivate our garden."'

It would be absurd to take the 'message' of *The Beloved Vagabond* more seriously than did the author. It would be

equally absurd not to take it seriously at all. The writer reflects
and plays cunningly with the daydreams of his huge middle-class
British audience. He understands the different *nuances* of those
daydreams. They are sometimes whimsical, laughable. But sometimes too, and this is heavily emphasized, they are to be regarded
as a form of quite serious philosophizing, a consideration of the
meaning of life. The daydreaming reader in London finds all
the philosophical options left happily open. For Paragot is a
kind of spiritual double agent. Asticot remarks that he had 'often
seen pierce through Paragot's travesty of mountebankery or rags
. . . the inborn and incommunicable quality of the high-bred
gentleman.' His gentlemanly instincts prevent him throwing himself entirely in with the cause of vagabondage; his high-toned
and well-tuned sense of freedom prevent his accepting the conventions of the gentleman. He betrays, so to speak, each side
in turn.

The repeated references to 'Reality' and 'Illusion' are characteristic of the period. It may be noted that the supposed
teachings of Indian philosophers, tailored to Western taste by
numerous gurus, were a popular fad among the British middle
classes of the time, as indeed they had been for many years
before and continued to be for many years after. It is more
or less traditional that in this kind of philosophizing a woman
such as Blanquette is more 'real' than a woman such as Joanna.
Similarly the country is in some way more real than the town.
When the country so described is the Sahara Desert, or a Pacific
island, it is usual to assume that its 'reality' consists in the fact
that it is not 'man-made' and by inference is God-made. But
this explanation, curious though it be, is not valid. In *The
Beloved Vagabond* and many other writings both in prose and
verse, well-tended expanses of agricultural or horticultural land
are, despite the visible evidences of human husbandry, nevertheless more real than Paris or London. Paragot escapes from the
'illusions' of conventional life on the one hand and Bohemian
vagabondage on the other to the 'reality' and 'truth' of his farm.
It would be oafish to enquire how, in his total ignorance of
farming methods and techniques, he proposes to make a go of
it. From a remark made by Blanquette about the necessity of
getting up at five in the morning to cut the corn, one may
deduce that Blanquette is his only farm-hand. The two of them
will have to manage not only the agriculture but the livestock,

12
Margaret Kennedy
Mansell Collection

13
Michael Arlen
*Radio Times Hulton
Picture Library*

14
Mary Webb
*Jonathan Cape
Limited*

15
Robert Keable
Mansell Collection

for it seems that Paragot sets a good deal of store by his possession of pigs. It is reassuring to the reader, and no doubt to Blanquette, that after buying the farm Paragot still has a little left of his capital. In any case we are certainly not intended to stand about waiting for a rainy day in Paragot's bucolic dreamland.

But even the reader most confident that he can eat his cake and have it can hardly hope that beneath the 'mountebankery or rags' of the Bohemian he will always find 'the inborn and incommunicable quality of the high-bred gentleman'.

Informed circles realize that the Bohemian is often not only a bit of a boor, but a bit of a cad. There are plenty of books in which this caddishness is noted for what it is and the caddish Bohemian exposed as unworthy of sympathy, still less of imitation or serious attention when he utters his outlandish remarks. But the door once shut in the face of these gate-crashers, the party is still not always satisfactory. It may lack *élan*, for it cannot be denied that, at least in literature, the presence of Bohemians, outsiders, even cads, can do a lot to make the party go. It is not too late to discover that the gate-crashers might after all be worthy of admittance. Uncouth they may be. The young ladies and, for all one knows, some of the young gentlemen may be in danger from their lascivious advances across the Edwardian or Georgian drawing-room. It is a matter of urgency for the host or hostess to explain that these people are carrying a little something extra under their unsuitable clothes. It may be just an Unconventional and Liberating view of Sex, or a Perception of Truth which no one else in the gathering happens to have about his person. More often, and more simply, what the Bohemians have is Genuis.

It is certainly a mark of general respect towards Art and Culture that anyone who is demonstrably a Genius in those lines finds, on walking into the pages of a popular novel, that everyone else is expected to overlook or at least try to condone his social *gaffes* and spiritual clangers. So far so good. But 'demonstrably' is the word which must necessarily bother the novelist. How to demonstrate the fact that the Genius has genius? On stage or film, and provided that the Genius is a musical one, the problem is simple. A top-notch musician can be engaged to write some pieces which the man can then play over as his own compositions on an electric piano. Even on stage or film, artists are more difficult to deal with, and writers are non-starters. It is not always enough for the rest of the characters to keep chattering about the beauty of the man's paintings. It is best to have someone come on with the news that his work has just been crowned with some exotic prize, or has sold for many thousands of guineas. The author with a genius as a character is near the position of a man trying to explain that *Hamlet* is a pretty good play to a man who has never heard of it. It is of little use to say, 'Well, here he asks himself the question whether to be or not to be, and goes on to make a long and marvellously poetic, marvellously philosophical speech.' The other man says, 'Well, fine, but what does he actually say?' Even if the man who is trying to put *Hamlet* over has memorized that one, he is going to be in trouble when he gets to the gravedigger scene or seeks to explain the play within the play. It is going to sound a lot of nonsense to the man he is trying to educate, and will not weigh much in the latter's opinion against the reports of how Shakespeare behaved to his wife and all those rumours about Mr W. H.

For the novelist to portray credibly a musical genius, or rather to make the fact of his genius credible to the reader, is a task of extraordinary difficulty. Yet it has been found necessary for him to do so. For it is necessary to resolve, or at least to clarify, the conflict in the mind of the reader between the respect he genuinely feels due to art, culture, and in a general sort of way 'the spiritual side of life', and 'everyday life' which means – again in a general sort of a way – getting or keeping money. Admittedly the genius and the Bohemian are not inevitably identical. One may again recall those artists observed by the vicar at St Ives. Still, as the genius often is a bit of a Bohemian, the fact has to be explained to the thoughtful bourgeois. And in any case the Bohemian, the vagabond, whether beloved or not, gradually becomes to some extent a welcome or unwelcome symbol of that 'spiritual side of life'. This was achieved partially by a negative process: that is to say, in so far as the Bohemian seemed to reject the conventions of a money-making society it had to be assumed that he was motivated by some immaterial inspiration which might be either divine or devilish.

Rank outsiders

THAT PHILISTINISM AND CULTURE are in some sort of conflict everyone can comfortably admit, knowing that the trouble is going to come later on when the members of the jury are asked to state just what they mean by Philistinism and what by Culture. But the fact that the conflict has been going on for ages, that the importance of local encounters is hard to assess, and that the battlefield is exceedingly confused, ought not to conceal the fact that there really is a battle.

On this ill-defined terrain, publication of Margaret Kennedy's *The Constant Nymph* was an action of significance. Published in 1924, it was the kind of book which would have given 'Old Puzzlehead' Sabre of *If Winter Comes* something to puzzle about : It was, to its credit, the kind of book about which people took sides, and about which Mark Sabre would hardly have known which side to take.

There is also a clear relation between its central social theme, which may be brutally encapsulated as the struggle of Art and Freedom against confining or debilitating Convention, and the problems of Paragot at Melford, Wilts.

To the paperback edition published in 1969 Margery Fisher has written a sympathetic, and useful, introduction. You may follow her on her brief guided tour around the book :

'I first read *The Constant Nymph* when I was fifteen. I have read it many times since then and have always been captured by its romantic charm, its gaiety and pathos. When it was first written, certain conventions, racial jokes and modes of behaviour were taken for granted (though not necessarily approved) which seems strange today. [This refers in part to *nuances* of anti-Semitism in the attitudes of several of the characters, particularly the children.] To some extent this novel has to be read as a period piece, rather as we read those parts of *The Forsyte Saga* which also reflect the 1920s. But *The Constant Nymph* has never been out of print and this means that it is relevant for any period.

Here is the story of fourteen-year-old Tessa, daughter of the flamboyant composer Albert Sanger and his second wife, a well-born Englishwoman. With her high benevolent forehead and "a kind of secret hilarity" in her greenish eyes, Tessa is happily innocent of convention, barely educated, physically fragile. She and her siblings – Antonia, Paulina, and Sebastian – share two principles in life : music and people's individuality are to be respected (music sometimes more than people). Sanger's two eldest children, Kate and Caryl, try to establish some order in the Tyrolese chalet which is the wandering family's only base, but Tessa has always accepted the noisy, unpredictable days at the Karindehuette as perfectly natural.

Death changes all this – the death of Albert Sanger. Instinctively, the four middle children turn to Lewis Dodd, a brilliant musician, ruthless in pursuit of his art, but genuinely devoted to the Sangers. As for Tessa, up till now he has been "our dear and beloved Lewis" who could be reviled or hugged without self-consciousness. Now, at fourteen she is full of doubts and fears, and tormented too by mysterious pains which, naturally, no Sanger could stop to notice.

Lewis has no more noticed Tessa's love for him than she has fully realized it. Soon the four ragamuffin children are taken to England by their cousin, to be "properly brought up". With them goes Lewis, so much captivated by the beautiful and accomplished Florence Churchill that he has made her his wife. Florence's good education has not taught her to understand people. She tries to groom Lewis for society stardom – Lewis, who, as Tessa sees, must be allowed to be himself, faults and all; and it is Tessa, the gawky schoolgirl, who offers a way to freedom through her honest and selfless love for him.

You do not have to read far in this novel to guess that Tessa is not destined for happiness. This is the tragedy of someone caught in circumstances which are bound to be fatal to them. But in the end Tessa is still unchanged, as free as she wanted Lewis to be, while Florence remains a prisoner in the narrow life she has chosen. It is the passionate integrity of Tessa that makes her tragedy real, and bearable for each generation of readers.'

It is true that *The Constant Nymph* is 'a period piece'. It is also true that its style is refreshing after long exposure to the style of the author's literary contemporaries. The plot, too, is more complex and the number of characters far greater than Margery Fisher has room to describe. As an exhibition of craftsmanship the author's construction-work is a pleasure to observe.

The introduction contains numerous key-words with which to open the various themes of the book. Tessa's mother is 'a well-born' Englishwoman. The goodness of her birth has an important bearing on the business. She died in 'dishonour, poverty and pain' brought upon her by Albert Sanger. Her two brothers had both distinguished themselves, the one being Principal of a flourishing university in the Midlands, the other the Master of a Cambridge college and 'acknowledged to be a great man by most of his generation'.

It is this background which ensures that Florence, as the cousin of Tessa and soon the wife of Lewis Dodd, shall be elected as representative of Conventional Values. Her values so far as background is concerned are disclosed almost immediately after she has agreed to marry the Bohemian Dodd, who is seen to have little if anything in the way of a social identity card. He proposes that when married they should live in England.

> ' "If you like," she said. "Your – your people live in England, don't they?"
>
> "My – Oh, yes!" he agreed, looking startled.
>
> "In London, you said?"
>
> "Yes."
>
> "I don't want to bother you to tell me if it is difficult, and nothing can make the slightest difference, but it is better for a wife to know, don't you think?"
>
> "Know what?"
>
> "What sort of people her husband belongs to. I haven't the vaguest idea about yours, Lewis, and you know all about mine."
>
> "My family are very disagreeable."
>
> "Yes?"
>
> "That's all."

"What do they consist of?"

"I have a father and a sister. My father was a school inspector, now he's a Member of Parliament. And he writes books. Two a year. Little text-books and outlines of things, for schools and working men who want to educate themselves, Science and English Literature and our Empire and those things."

"Oh! can he – is he – any relation to Sir Felix Dodd?"

"He is Sir Felix Dodd."

"W –what?"

"He is Sir Felix Dodd."

She was petrified with astonishment and could only sit gaping at him.

"Know him?" he asked pleasantly.

"My father knows him."

"I am sorry for your father, then."

She knew that Charles hated Sir Felix Dodd; he was always abusing him. They sat on many boards together, for the School Inspector M.P. was a power in the educational world. Charles had dubbed him Fulsome Felix and avoided him as far as possible.

"Good heavens, Lewis," she stammered. "I can't . . . I never . . . how very strange! I never knew Sir Felix had a son, at least . . ."

She remembered now she had heard of a son who was a terrible scamp and was not to be mentioned in the presence of anybody connected with the Dodds. What nonsense people talk!

Lewis for his peace of mind did not grasp the full significance of it. It did not seem to him very important that Florence already knew about his people. He said impatiently that he had quite lost touch with them and she wisely let the subject drop. Later on she would make him tell her what the trouble had been, and then when they returned to England she would smooth it all out. They must be brought to forgive him, whatever he had done.

For herself this news was a great blessing. She would not after all be forced to scandalise her family. She was radiant as they set off for the station, feeling that life had been very good to her.

"I would have married him", she thought, "if his father had been hangman, but this does make a difference." '

In contrast to Cousin Florence, Tessa is 'innocent of convention'. In fact, and this is significant of the period, she is unconventional only in the mildest sense, except in the central and vital matter of her fixation on Lewis Dodd. Naturally one of her 'principles in life' is 'individuality', but her individuality is expressed almost entirely in her fourteen-year-old passion for the adult Bohemian. But for the greater part of the book her sister Antonia appears as a very much more vivid character, acting in, if one may so put it, a conventionally unconventional manner.

'This eldest of Evelyn's children was by far the most handsome; she was born before retribution had fully overtaken her mother, and did not look as delicate as the rest. She was full of changeful colour and brilliance though her bloom was just beginning and she still had the coltlike movements, the long limbs and loose joints of a very young creature. To the experienced eyes her promise was infinite ... In character she also resembled her mother; was unbalanced, proud and at times impossibly generous. But she lacked Evelyn's courage, and was reckless rather than intrepid. She could only take a risk by deceiving herself as to its issue, and confronted by reality she always went to pieces. She cried when she could not get what she wanted, boasted when she was frightened, and was, like her sisters, a deplorable little slattern.'

For a lark Antonia runs away from the family home at the Karindehuette and goes to Munich to become the mistress of a rich Jew called Jacob Birnbaum whom she refers to 'on account of his nose and cheek bones' as 'Ikey Mo'. She spends a week there making love, eating enormous and expensive meals, and drinking quantities of champagne. She leaves abruptly for the reason that she wants to be back for Sanger's birthday. Later, after Sanger's death, she returns to Birnbaum and after firing a hail of crackling insults at him agrees to marry him. She is not doing so for his money. His money he reflects, makes very little difference to her.

'He had seen that in Munich and it had continually exasperated him. For though she had snatched at the good things he gave her he could not persuade himself that he had bought her. She would take nothing away with her, scorning his lavish offers of clothes and jewels. It was the Sanger spirit of conviviality which brought her. She would have been quite as ready to enjoy herself if he had been a poor man; if he had lodged her in a garret and taken her to the cinema instead of the opera.

It was this lordly relish for life, a fiery abundance of spirit enriching everything in its orbit, which had first attracted him to Sanger. He now saw it repeated in Sanger's children. To himself money had always meant too much. It pervaded his entire existence, intervening and robbing him of the full fruits of experience. It had furnished him with all his assets, his pleasures and the positions he held in the musical world. In moments of depression he was inclined to fear that it had provided his friendships; he used to wonder how many people would have tolerated him without it. He had the instincts of a patriarch and would have liked to beget children and found a family, a household, but he had purchased so many women that he despaired of finding one who was not venal. His short association with Tony had taught him that she was neither sensual nor mercenary, and that in her least thought she was guided by an impulse which had been denied to him. She demanded only to feel; she asked of life only that it should play a tune to her dancing. A queer wife she would be! a darling wife!'

We reach the central fact : Lewis Dodd is 'brilliant', 'ruthless in pursuit of his art', and 'has no more noticed Tessa's love for him than she has fully realized it.' Of this ruthlessness must be said that a great deal of it has to be taken for granted. The deceased Sanger is well documented as being pretty much of a brute – particularly in his relations with women. Lewis Dodd's ruthlessness takes for the most part the form of rather schoolboy rudeness to and about people whose musical taste he considers inferior to his own, displays of petty selfishness, and explosions of ill-temper – usually on occasions when ill-temper seems well justified. More importantly there is his singularly obtuse insensivity to Tessa's emotional condition in relation to himself.

Before his marriage to Florence, Tessa's twelve-year-old sister Paulina urges Tessa to ask Dodd to marry her. 'He is very nice,' says Paulina. 'I would ask him myself only he loves you best.'

' "I am too young."

"Not a bit, you can ask him, anyhow."

"Oh I couldn't, I'm too old."

"Too old? I thought you said you were too young!"

"So I did. Dear me! I am both, I am a perfectly horrid age. I am too old to say what I think and I am too young for anybody to want to marry me."

"There, now you are blushing again. You'll be worse than Kate soon. She used to blush regularly; I mean always at the same sort of thing. But you have taken to blushing at nothing at all, you're dreadful."

"You wait until you're my age. You will too."

"Still, I can't see why you should think you are too young for Lewis. You would suit him much better than that ordinary woman who expects him always to be bothering about her . . ."

"Would I? Look!"

They were sitting at the edge of the forest near the bottom of the mountain. Tessa pointed to the bottom of the field below them where two figures were strolling intimately [they are of course Lewis Dodd and Florence]. Paulina took them in and asked anxiously:

"Do you think he wants her?"

Tessa nodded.

"But he wouldn't marry her!" protested Paulina.

"Yes, he will. She'll make him."

"He has never married anybody before."

"Yes, but she's a lady. If it's anybody like Florence they have to marry them. Look at Sanger and our mother."

"But she won't have him," persisted Paulina hopefully. "Why should she? Think of all the grand people she knows. She's just being nice to him like she is to everybody."

"I wouldn't mind his getting her," said Tessa sadly, "if that was all there was to it, but that will only be the beginning, you see! She will want to take him off and live at that place in England where she comes from, Cambridge. He won't be happy."

"I think it will be a shame if he gets her. She can't have seen him drunk."

"Of course she hasn't. He's not been drunk since she came."

"And she can't have seen him in a temper. Really in lots of ways worse than Sanger. He's not so good-natured for one thing. Tessa, do you think we ought to tell her?"

"Tell her what?"

"That it wouldn't do at all. There are heaps of things – "

"I can't," said Tessa, who had gone very pale.

"Why not? If she knew – "

"I don't know why not, but I couldn't."

"Well, it would be rather like telling tales. He belongs to us, really, more than she does. Perhaps she'll find out herself."

This was said in a very low voice as the pair were quite close to them. They were picking flowers of different sorts and saying at intervals they had got enough and then crying out over a good one that must be picked.

"Oh," cried Florence, flinging herself down on the grass by the girls, "did you ever see such flowers? they beat even the Academy pictures of 'Spring in the Austrian Tyrol'."

"What are you going to do with these little things?" asked Lewis, dropping gentians into her lap, one by one.

"Put them in a dish of moss on the hall table."

"Very tasteful! Tessa! Why have we never put dishes of gentians on the hall table before?"

"Because we don't want them," said Tessa coldly.'

The degree of Lewis Dodd's Bohemianism does not matter; what matters for the novelist is its impact upon the members of conventional society. On the news of Dodd's engagement to his niece, her uncle Robert, the one who is Principal of the flourishing university in the Midlands exclaims, 'Who could have thought that Florence, a sensible woman like Florence, not quite a young girl either, would dream of doing such a thing? A delicate-minded, well bred girl to take up with a wretched mountebank, a disagreeable, ill-conditioned young cub with the manners of – of – Well, he hasn't got any manners, and goodness knows if he ever washes.'

' "Oh, but he does!" interrupted Antonia, recovering speech. "I am sure he does, Uncle Robert, I've seen him."

"Well, he doesn't look as if he does. A shoddy Bohemian! One of those bad-blooded young ruffians who defy decency and call it art. No better than a hooligan! Oh, yes, I daresay he has done some very fine work, but that is no reason why she should want to marry him. Good heavens! isn't it enough to have had one of them in the family? Couldn't she have been warned? I should have thought the look of him would be sufficient; a sulky impudent-looking fellow who's probably sprung from the gutter, without a single . . . "

"You are mistaken, Mr Churchill," put in Jacob Birnbaum. "I think that his family is very good. His father is Sir Felix Dodd. You have heard of him . . . yes?"

"Dodd! Dodd! Good God!" spluttered Uncle Robert.

Jacob hastily produced all the details in his possession which could cast any light on Lewis's early career. Uncle Robert continued to call at intervals upon Dodd and God.

"But what on earth can they think they are doing?" asked Antonia. "They must be mad. Florence is so clever. And Lewis isn't, a bit. And she's very good too . . . "

"But," broke in her uncle, "but to my mind this about his family makes it worse. Much worse! There must have been some very grave scandal before an English family would cut off . . . "

"I do not believe there was a scandal," said Jacob, "and I think that he cut them off. I never heard that this was their wish. He ran away because he did not like his father. He has lived a wandering life but I think there has been no disgrace. I know he played the cornet once, with a circus . . . "

"Completely *déclassé*," groaned Uncle Robert. "No, I think his possessing a family makes it worse. I remember now, I did hear that old Dodd had a scamp of a son who had run away from school. A tramp! A circus band! You tell me that he had the education and the opportunities of a gentleman, and threw them away to play the cornet in a circus band? Then there is nothing to be said for him as far as I can see. I shall go out and telegraph. I shall wire to Florence that I don't approve at all. I shall entreat her father to come out and stop it."

Tea hardly pacified him. He swallowed a little and then bustled off to despatch his telegram. Jacob and Antonia mournfully discussed the event.

"She can't know what he is really like," said Antonia.

"It is madness," agreed Jacob. "He has cut himself off from her world because he will not endure it. Will he now return to it? or does he think that she will share his life?"

Antonia conjectured that Florence did not know very much about his life. She remembered a conversation in which his name had been mentioned and said :

"I think she rather admires his character."

"Admires!"

"Yes. She said he was – what was it? An ascetic! what does that mean?"

"It means a man who will practise a life of austerity for the cause of some great ideal," he told her.

"O-o-oh! But . . . "

"You would say that this does not describe Lewis?"

"I never knew him go without anything he wanted."

"Nor I. It is true that he does not want very much. Perhaps she admires him for that. A wild savage would want even less than he does. Yet she would not marry a wild savage. In some ways Lewis is not so much to be admired as a wild savage." '

In Uncle Robert's attitude we have an entertainingly sketched caricature of what might be called the conventional view of the unconventional. One may assume that there really were innumerable members of the middle class who really would have acted and spoken as does Uncle Robert, but it may equally be assumed that not many of them would read *The Constant Nymph*. Uncle Robert's attack on the Bohemian is to be seen as the author's defence of him. Very few readers would identify with Uncle Robert. The majority is left with the comfortable conviction that it is not as Philistine as all that. It could be said that to this extent the bout of Art v. Culure is a sham fight – it has been rigged in advance. But then a question obtrudes itself.

If *The Constant Nymph* is to be read as 'a period piece', and thus to some extent a report on the manners and customs of a period, then is it not possible that the fight was not so phoney after all; that a large number of the readers were sufficiently of Uncle Robert's way of thinking to get a genuine jolt when they saw their faces in the mirror of the book? Did not *The Constant Nymph*, therefore, with the skill of its writing, strike a genuine blow against British Philistinism?

If everyone old enough to have read it on publication were to declare freely and frankly just what effect it had upon him or herself, and their contemporaries, these questions would be answered. Unfortunately the difficulties of conducting such an opinion poll are insuperable. In his admirable book from which I have already quoted, *The Rise of the Novel*, Professor Ian Watts writes: 'It is one of the general difficulties in applying social history to the interpretation of literature that, uncertain as our knowledge of any particular social change may be, our knowledge of its objective aspects, the way it affected the thoughts and feelings of the individuals concerned, is even more insecure and hypothetical, yet the problem cannot altogether be avoided.'

It is a problem which legitimately teases the reader who, while appreciating the excellent literary qualities of *The Constant Nymph*, still wants to know whether, less than fifty years ago, people's attitudes, notably towards sex, were really what the book seems to say they were. I say 'legitimately' because, for all its lightness of touch, *The Constant Nymph* was a 'social novel' and was discussed seriously as such. The central theme is the relationship between Lewis Dodd and the girl Tessa. It is in fact this rather than his supposedly ruthless dedication to his art which determines Lewis Dodd's behaviour. It is the basic cause of the divisions between himself and his wife Florence. Tessa, with Lewis Dodd's original approval, has been sent to a 'good' English school. She finds it intolerable and runs away. Lewis is determined that she shall not be sent back to it, Florence that she shall.

'Always they seemed to fight about such foolish things. This time it was the old wretched question of Teresa's future. Lewis was determined that the child should not go to school again. He spoilt her outrageously. For the other two a settlement seemed possible but about Teresa there was no agreeing. The fight became unbelievably fierce and Florence noticed an inflection in her voice which reminded her of the railings of Linda Cowlard. She fell silent, horrified and ashamed, and Lewis got in the last word.

"If Tessa leaves this house," he vowed, "I leave it. She is the only thing that makes life tolerable, so I warn you!"'

One gets just a whiff of the problem presented to Mr and Mrs Sabre when Mark Sabre insists on 'little Effie' sharing the house with them. At this point neither Lewis Dodd nor Florence appears to know much about what is really the matter with Tessa. She is suffering from heart-disease in both senses of the term. They know that her mother died of heart-disease and they have a school medical report showing that Tessa herself suffers from a 'valvular lesion' which prevents her playing hockey. They attribute her consequent symptoms to growing sickness. They are equally ignorant of the nature and effects of Tessa's fourteen-year-old infatuation for Dodd, her fixation upon him. None of the other adults seem to take it seriously either. Her sisters appear more clear-sighted. (This belief in the superior vision of children is not one peculiar to the early 1920s. The device has often been used before and since as a convenient way of spotlighting the degree to which adults have become blinded to basic realities by their involvement in everyday life.) Certainly Lewis Dodd was not in a position to have heard of *Lolita*, and the word 'nymphet' was not in use in his time. Still the phenomenon of a girl in her early teens obsessed and in love with a much older man cannot have been uncommon in the 1920s and cannot always have been laughed off as a 'schoolgirl crush'. The fact that Lewis Dodd has never heard of such a thing seems to indicate not so much excessive absorption in his art as a dimwitted ignorance strange in a young man who, one is given to understand, has had a fairly wide range of sexual experience. For this ignorance there are two possible explanations : The first is the censorship, overt and otherwise, notably the half-invisible censorship exercised by the circulating libraries. Perhaps a less kid-gloved treatment of Tessa's condition would have been shocking. Perhaps a majority of the readers knew quite well that in real life Dodd would have at least recognized the problem and might, even at that date, have called in a psychiatrist. But it could have been accepted that the kid-glove treatment was essential if the book were not to be threatened with action as liable to deprave or corrupt. So open an admission that there was a sexual basis for Tessa's emotions might have been judged to do just that.

Alternatively it could be held that another and deeper kind of censorship was at work. It can be that a majority of the readers really did not want to look too steadily at the sexual aspects of the situation. So far as a majority of readers were concerned the latter explanation seems the more likely. Otherwise how would they have accepted without bewilderment the scene very late in the book when first Lewis Dodd and then his wife admit to what to everyone else has for long been an increasingly obvious fact? Having decided to leave his wife (and Tessa) and go off on his own, Lewis suddenly appears in a frame of mind more like that of Mark Sabre than one would have thought possible in a man of such sharply different experience. He has just said goodbye to Tessa – though privately notifying her that he is going by the

early boat to Brussels in case she might feel disposed to slip out of
the house next morning and join him.

He seems not to suppose that Tessa will take him seriously, for
a few minutes later he is thinking and talking on the assumption
that he is leaving her as well as Florence. Alone with Florence,

'He was seized with a strong, sudden impulse to deal openly
with her. To lay the whole truth before her and to trust that
the truth might mend matters. The truth to him was the story
of Tessa's goodness, her sweet staunch loyalty. There had been
some baseness and enmity between the three of them, but none
of it had touched Tessa and he scarcely believed that it could
live if it was brought into the light. He was going away. He
had to leave his love behind him. It seemed to him that he
might endure that if Florence would but comprehend her. He
turned round and said to her with a new grave friendliness :
"I wish that you would be better friends with Tessa – that
you would love her. She deserves to be loved. Everybody must,
I think, that really knows her. If you could hear how she
speaks of you how she admires you, you . . . couldn't help it. I
don't think you quite understand how . . . how good she is."

"No . . . I don't quite understand," she said with a bitterness
which in his eager appeal he failed to remark.

"I can't bear to go away and leave her with people who
don't know that," he said simply. "Do try, Florence. I know I
am a bad advocate. I know I behaved very badly to you. This
has been a wretched business and it is best that I should go
away. I have only made you unhappy and I shall go on making
you unhappy. But I feel that the worst thing I have done is
that somehow I have put you and Tessa against each other.
Because you ought to love each other. My fault that is! I have
not spoken plainly. You see . . . I love her so much . . . so
much! I want to know that she will be happy. And now I
have to leave her with you and you treat her as if she were an
enemy. She is not. What can I say? You are so much better
fitted to love each other, you two, than I am to have anything
to do with either of you. Oh Florence, can't you see it? If you
would only see it I could go away and say God bless you
both !''

She had not thought it possible that he could speak like this.
In all their life together she had never heard these tones in his

voice or met that look of unreserved appeal, save once in the Tyrol when he first spoke to her of the little girls and begged her to take them to England. She had loved him for that hour. And now she knew that it was all for Teresa, the gentleness which she had divined in him then. She had given her heart to Teresa's lover.

"Since when have you loved her so terribly?"

He didn't know. Always, he supposed.

"Why then did you marry me?"

"I was a fool. Oh Florence, be angry with me, not with her! She's done nothing to deserve it. She loves you."

"Have you told her? Does she know?"

"Yes, she knows, and you knew it too, didn't you? Didn't you? You've known it for a long time. That is why I am speaking of her now, because you know it already and you're a person one can dare speak the truth to. And you were angry because I didn't tell it, weren't you? You thought you deserved straighter dealings. And now you see that it isn't her fault. You're too generous to do anything else . . . " '

Florence flings at him 'the question which for weeks had tormented her, returning to her mind as often as she banished it'. Thus it is only 'for weeks' that the thought of a sexual factor in the relationship between Lewis and Tessa has occurred to her.

' "You may as well tell the whole truth now. What exactly has there been between you?"

"I told you. I love her."

"And what does that mean? Is she your mistress?"

Though she could not look at him she could feel the shock of his sudden anger, but he tried to control himself.

"No, she is not. I tell you, she will have nothing to do with me because she loves you."

"I don't believe you."

"It's true. She would never be as unjust to you."

"What am I to believe? I have seen enough of the whole pack of you to know that you can't be trusted." '

Lewis slams out of the house. Hearing him go, Tessa has bad pains in her chest. Florence administers sal volatile. She then makes a violent scene accusing Tessa of shamelessly pursuing

Lewis. Her anger is so ugly and alarming that Tessa rushes from the house in turn, on the verge of suicide. In a distracted change of mind she sends a note to Dodd instead saying that after all she will meet him on the morning boat train.

The closing scenes in a squalid Brussels boarding house are so simple, so moving, so credible, in any terms regardless of 'period', as to seem strangely out of key with that earlier sequence in which Lewis and Florence so abruptly and, in the dramatic sense of the word, so catastrophically admit what must seem to the reader the obvious facts of life. The reader may be forced to the conclusion that the sequence, too, was credible to the author and her readers, that this was something which really could have occurred in the early 1920s.

Paradoxically, the book-buying public of the day put at the top of its list of essential reading Michal Arlen's *The Green Hat*. Paradoxically, because there can hardly have been an England more unrecognizably different from that to which Florence brought Lewis Dodd and Tessa than the land phosphorescent with the brilliance of decay through which the young Armenian, after a sporting failure to imitate Arnold Bennett, led a horde of entranced, shocked or derisive sight-seers. In fact one more game in the long series of Bohemia v. The Rest is being played here too.

The heroine is a Bohemian and very much at odds with her environment. In an early statement about herself, immediately after being with the narrator, she remarks : 'It is not good to have a pagan body and a Chislehurst mind, as I have. It is hell for the body, and terror for the mind. There are dreams, and there are beasts. The dreams walk glittering up and down the soiled loneliness of desire, the beasts prowl about the soiled loneliness of regret.'

The narrator, too, is a Bohemian, an outsider. And central to the book is his love-hate relationship with, in the first place, England and, at a different level, the *haute bourgeoisie* of dying Western society.

The book can be and indeed often was read as an elaborate floral tribute laid by an adulatory foreigner at the feet of the Old Raj. Aristocrats of amazingly rigid principles stalk the book, often giving the impression of splendid figures who, with no sansculottes available, have to operate their own guillotines.

Speaking of 'the England I love' the narrator soliloquizes:

'I am not sure that I can explain what that England is. I
am not sure that I would like to explain it even to myself, as,
maybe for the same reason, I would not like to read Jane
Austen with a mental measure. I am not sure that there is such
an England, that there ever was such an England. The soil, to
be sure, is there, the clouds across the sun, the teasing humours
of the island seasons: the halls, the parklands, the spacious
rooms, they are there. But the figures that sweep across them
– are these that we see, all? Are there no others, lost somewhere, calmly ready to show themselves – are these that we
see all? These healthy, high-busted women with muscles like
minotaurs, these girls who are either stunned with health or
pale with the common vapours of common dance-halls, these
stout, graceless ones here, those too slender bloodless ones
there, these things that have no voice between a shout and a
whisper, these things that have yielded to democracy nothing
but their dignity – are these that we see, all? These rather
caddish young men who have no vision between a pimply
purity and vice, who are without the grace with which to
adorn ignorance or the learning with which to make vulgarity
tolerable, these peasant-minded noblewomen, these matrons
who appear to have gained in youth what they have lost
in dignity, these toiling dancers, these elderly gentlemen with their ungallant vices – are these that we see, all? Or
was there never such an England? Were the parklands and the
spacious rooms never peopled but by nincompoops let loose
by wealth among the graces of learning and fashion?'

The theme recurs in rather more spritely manner, in relation
to the predecessors of the jet set (here we are in Paris).

'The Place Vendôme is, therefore, no place for a plain man,
nor by any means a safe station for the man in the street:
there are motor-cars kept in readiness to run them over . . .
And always the great column on which Napoleon stands rises
to the clouds, but no one cares about that. All they care about
are the forty-eight automobiles and one coach-and-six which
stretch, in ordered array of two lines, from the foot of his
column to the entrance of the Ritz. The shops are loaded

with diamonds as large as carnations and with carnations as
expensive as diamonds. The shop-keepers are very polite, and
courteously do not mind how many you buy. Americans buy.
Englishmen watch the Americans buying. Grand Dukes wait
for the Englishmen to dare them to have a cocktail. A few
Frenchmen are stationed at strategic points where they can
best be rude to the English and Americans. Then the English
and Americans tip them. The women do not wear stays and
insist on their men shaving twice a day.'

The readers of *The Green Hat* could have everything both
ways. They could follow their guide, so gay, so debonair, with
such an extravagant gift of the gab, through the brilliantly lit
or darkly lurid premises of an imaginary aristocracy, identifying
the agreeable with the beautiful, the high-born, and the damned.
And then, just as they might begin to feel some sense of guilt
at their own enjoyment of the spectacle, the guide strips off
his white tie and tails, grinds his frivolous monocle under
a stern heel, and reveals himself momentarily in the garb of a
Minor Old English Prophet, rebuking the vanity of it all, and
sonorously lamenting the passing of the Old Virtues, the Old
Values, the Old Conventions.

Apart from having a Chislehurst mind in a pagan body, Iris
the heroine is an outcast from her caste, principally because with
aristocratic chivalry she refuses to disclose the true reason for her
husband's suicide on their wedding night. It was that he realized
that he had syphilis. All Iris will say is that 'he died for purity.'
This his friends take to mean that it was her her own impurity
which shocked him. And since he was an idolized caste-member,
Iris is spurned or treated with suspicious contempt.

As a result, she goes, not to put too fine a point on it, off the
rails. In the end the caste-members realize that they have made
a terribly mistaken judgement about her. But it is too late so far
as Iris is concerned. She has dashed herself to death in a great
car against a symbolic type of oak tree, in order not to ruin the
love-life of the girl who is in love with the man who is in love
with Iris.

Fortunately the plot matters very little. It serves principally as
a hurriedly constructed though highly painted vehicle in which
the reader is to be taken on the conducted tour through an
imaginary England. But since the tour immediately became

immensely popular and was heavily over-booked at the circulating libraries of two continents, it was clearly an imaginary England which enormous numbers of people at least wanted to
believe in.

There were critics who deemed the book shockingly vulgar,
tawdry, meretricious, and – more helpfully – immoral, glistening
with nasty bits of phosphorescence borrowed from the decadent
Nineties. Not many people will admit that what they sometimes
feel the need of, by way of a good read, is something vulgarly
tawdry and immorally meretricious. There are, nevertheless,
many indeed who do feel that way. Some such certainly helped
to launch the book, along with those others who were excited by
the views of favourable critics who noted the book's originality,
stylistic coruscations, and 'refreshing candour' in relation to 'sub-
jects normally taboo'. (Crude customers automatically translated
this last phrase into the words 'bloody hot stuff' and 'a bit of you-
know-what'.)

Whichever of the qualities mentioned any given member of the
public was in search of, he (meaning especially she) was not
disappointed. And those who curled up with *The Green Hat* were
immediately caressed and flattered by the author's blandly
chosen sub-title : 'A Romance for a Few People'. A book, in fact,
exclusively for you and me and only a few hundred thousand
others.

The snob appeal was splendidly blatant. Although plenty of
native writers could put it over well, perhaps only an Armenian
would have dared to bet so confidently on Western middle-class
snobbery, and to nurse it along so adroitly.

Apart from the narrator, the first character to appear in the
book is not a human being but a motor-car: 'a long, low, yellow
car which shone like a battle chariot. Now I am of those who are
affected by motor-cars.' So, of course, were huge numbers of
potential readers. In the nineteen-twenties (as Dornford Yates so
shrewdly and profitably realized) the motor-car was still capable
of being, so to speak, a major member of the cast, only just inferior in importance and allure to the Hero and Heroine.

But the car standing in Shepherd Market at the beginning of
Arlen's book was something rather special.

'Like a huge yellow insect that had dropped to earth from
a butterfly civilization, this car, gallant and suave, rested in the

lowly silence of the Shepherd's Market [*sic*] night. Open as a yacht, it wore a great shining bonnet, and flying over the crest of this great bonnet, as though in proud flight over the heads of scores of phantom horses, was that silver stork by which the gentle may be pleased to know that they have just escaped death beneath the wheels of a Hispano-Suiza car, as supplied to His Most Catholic Majesty.'

The breadth of Michael Arlen's appeal was attested by the fact that he, born Dikran Kouyoumdjian, was, I believe, the only novelist to have his trouser-buttons torn off by mobs of fans on the quay at New York. That had happened earlier to film stars, and was to happen later to pop-singers, but not to novelists.

Nor was the fame of *The Green Hat* known in the Western world only. Michael Arlen himself once told me that some time after the explosion of *The Green Hat* he was crossing a section of Asia Minor in a motor-coach. (The coach was then the missing link between two airports.) At some point along the route, the well-heeled occupants of the coach were at first surprised, then much alarmed, to note that the driver had left the already miserable road, and was heading up a sidetrack, which could have been a dried-up watercourse.

The passengers naturally supposed themselves about to be robbed, kidnapped, and held to ransom, or murdered on the spot.

On reaching a huge pile of rocks, biblical in its solemnity, the driver halted the coach, and invited the passengers to get out. Clutching wallets and jewellery they did so. The driver said : 'Ladies and gentlemen, I am an Armenian. You of the West know little of the grandeur of our people. I have therefore brought you here to see with your own eyes the noble tomb of one of the greatest and most resplendent of Armenian thinkers, story-tellers and poets – Dikran Kouyoumdjian. Such are the monuments we raise to our glorious dead. I am sure you will all look upon it with proper reverence.'

Dikran Kouyoumdjian and his fellow-passengers did so, though the others could not be aware that the emotions of this Mr Arlen were different from their own.

A sense of grievance

'... Reprinted 1928 (five times), 1929 (three times), 1930 (twice), 1931, 1932 (three times), 1933 (three times), 1934, 1935 (twice), 1937, 1938, 1939 (twice), 1941, 1942, 1943, 1945, 1947, 1949, 1953, 1956, 1957, 1963, 1967 ...'

The figures reveal part of the story of how Mary Webb's fine novel, *Precious Bane*, rose to fame and stayed there. The rest of the story, sometimes very dolorous, is also revealing: it tells much about mysterious changes of public taste, the literary life, and the undefined role of luck in the creation of a best-seller. The whole affair is as vivid, bizarre, and reflective as the book itself. Like the book it contains elements which might strike a cool critic as corny, underlining the fact that real life is often somewhat cornier than fiction, of a kind less audacious than Mary Webb's, would dare to be.

She was born in 1881, daughter of a schoolmaster, and later married to a schoolmaster in very rural Shropshire. At the age of thirty-five she published her first novel. Nobody noticed. Next year she published her second, *Gone To Earth*. Rebecca West perspicaciously picked it out of the ruck and acclaimed it as 'the novel of the year'. Hardly anyone bought it. The next two novels were complete flops. The fifth was *Precious Bane*. As an almost least-selling novelist, she had to accept from the publisher Jonathan Cape an advance of only one hundred pounds. Michael S. Howard, son of Cape's partner, G. Wren Howard, in his history of the firm, takes up the story:

'At the end of the first year the book had still sold less than fifteen hundred copies, and had not earned three-quarters of the hundred pounds advance. Meanwhile Mary Webb was importuning Cape for more advances against royalties, and even for petty loans – which she was then unable to repay. She felt a sense of grievance about money. Writing earlier to a friend, she had complained that the British public did not pay fairly for her work, "so that I have this week existed on bread and scrape and tea." '

Assuming that she knew, as she almost certainly did, that she had written the finest novel of the day, a book of unique and admirable character, one need not see anything neurotic or paranoid about that 'sense of grievance about money'. But one wonders what pathetically Utopian concept she had of a society in which 'the public' would pay 'fairly'.

In addition to her other troubles, she, who would otherwise have been an exceptionally good-looking woman, was afflicted with a goitre and a harelip. The goitre she could conceal with scarves, but not the harelip.

'She was not strong,' Howard goes on, 'yet while living in the country she had kept a stall in Shrewsbury market, nine miles from her home, and would rise at three in the morning to pick flowers from her garden, walk with them to Shrewsbury, and sell them there for a halfpenny a bunch.'

But writers and artists are notoriously feckless about money.

'As soon as she earned money she gave it away with both hands – a hundred pounds to move a consumptive boy from the East End to the seaside; food, clothes, and money to any down-and-out who came begging at her door. Then she became desperate for her own needs, to keep in touch with literary friends and attend gatherings in London; so she besieged her publishers. She asked Cape for part-time reading work. He had none to offer, and declined to make her any further loans. She came to 30 Bedford Square, an immense bow of tulle tied about her neck below the frightened-looking little face. Jonathan was otherwise engaged, so she saw Howard [the partner] and tried to persuade him to let her have more money. He refused. In petulant rage she slapped his face, and swept out of the office.'

As Michael Howard records, 'a few discerning critics had judged *Precious Bane* a masterpiece', and in 1925 it was awarded the Femina Vie Heureuse prize 'for the best work of imagination in prose or verse descriptive of English life'. But the sales remained minuscule. A distinguished reviewer explained the situation by remarking that her work was 'not sufficiently in the spirit of our time to awaken more than literary interest'.

This judgement poses some interesting questions. Just what was this 'spirit of our time' which, to the reviewer, seems to have been definable, nearly palpable? Probably the most important literary event of the period was the appearance of Hemingway on the British literary scene. T. E. Lawrence's *The Seven Pillars of Wisdom* was in great demand. Travel books of a politico-philosophical nature were, among big sections of the reading public, more popular than fiction. But looking back it is hard to detect with any clarity that 'spirit'. More important: if that reviewer was right (and Mary Webb's sales seem to indicate that he was), then how is it that the spirit changed so radically that within a few years it carried her to the top of the best-seller lists and kept her there for years and years? As will be seen, Stanley Baldwin, Conservative Premier, did much to introduce Webb to the spirit. But although he could launch her, he could hardly have kept her in orbit for such a very long time.

The phrase about the books being unlikely to 'awaken more than literary interest' is curiously suggestive. It is easy to say that one 'sees what the man meant'. But, since the phrase was in common use, it would have been instructive if those who used it had spelled it out more clearly. Did it, does it when used today, mean that the 'story', and the 'characters', and the setting, may awaken general interest, but that qualities of style and construction cannot hope to attract more than literary interest, that literary men alone will be interested in them? It is a belief widely held by general readers; they 'read the book for the story', they say, and claim not to bother about style and construction. The writer is not bound to advertise his stylistic and constructional abilities. He need not, often – perhaps should not – seem to be pointing and calling out: 'See me make with the verbiage. Watch me weave the themes.' But the general reader who supposes he is very plainly and simply being rattled along by the yarn is in reality gripped, guided, and sometimes hallucinated by the skills of 'purely literary interest'.

The injection of ostentatiously bucolic iron-master and politician Stanley Baldwin into the situation could appear grotesque. On the other hand, perhaps this shrewd and slippery

Tory boss, who managed to represent himself to millions as the archetype of a bumbling but supremely honest chap, oop frum Zummerzet, or Shropshire, for the good of the country, really was a valid emanation of the spirit of the time.

Things so fell out (it seems the right phrase) that Hamish Hamilton, the publisher and a devotee of Mary Webb, kept talking about her at a little dinner party at which was present the powerful Tom Jones, Deputy-Secretary to the Cabinet. Gathering that *Precious Bane* had to do with the Shropshire border, where the Baldwin family were proud of having lived for centuries, Jones said to Hamilton, 'That sounds the sort of thing that would interest the P.M.' Hamilton, proving vigorously loyal to Mary Webb's interests, sent the book to Jones, asking him to give it to Baldwin, which Jones did. Baldwin read it over Christmas, sent Mary Webb a note to say how much he had enjoyed it, and she sent him back her thanks and a bunch of violets.

A few months later her always feeble body broke down altogether. She died, frustrated and in the black depths of disappointment at the almost total public indifference to her books.

It would take a clairvoyant to name, among the ingredients that were to prove essential to the making of this particular bestseller, a man's outstanding proficiency in rowing. But the facts, a good deal too improbable for fiction, were that Hamish Hamilton was a leading oarsman and a member of the British rowing team competing in the Olympic Games at Amsterdam in 1928; that on the eve of the Olympics the crew entertained Baldwin, in the capacity of ex-officio lover of British sport, to lunch; that Hamilton sat next to the Prime Minister and talked to him about *Precious Bane*; and that Baldwin said he would like to speak about the book at a dinner of the Royal Literary Fund in April.

Baldwin was as good as his word, in itself a rare tribute to the impact of Mary Webb. He did speak at the dinner, and in the course of his speech said that he had not relied on his own opinion alone but had consulted both Sir James Barrie and John Buchan. 'They told him', records Howard, 'that they regarded her as one of the best British writers then alive, but that no one bought her books. The Prime Minister's public utterance succeeded where the efforts of distinguished critics had all failed, and the neglected masterpiece became a bestseller overnight.' The principal credit for this outcome must certainly go to the indefatigable Hamish Hamilton.

It should just be mentioned that in some limited circles the utterance was counter-productive. I recall from personal experience that sections of the young intelligentsia took the view that if Stanley Baldwin liked a book it must be about the vilest bit of non-literature ever printed. Nor did mention of Barrie and Buchan much help. If the word 'square', in its later meaning, had been in use at the time, 'those old squares' would have been what Barrie and Buchan would have been referred to as nothing else but.

No one can suppose that Baldwin alone was responsible for the prolonged best-selling of *Precious Bane*. Still, it is of significance that incalculable numbers of people did buy or borrow the book solely on his recommendation. We (I refer to the young intelligentsia) would have found it natural enough that the British counterparts of Mencken's *booboisie* should be stirred by 'honest Stan' to sheepish admiration of some philistine mess of a book. It would have seemed a contradiction in terms that the third point of the triangle Baldwin–public–book should be positively good.

Baldwin followed up his speech with an introduction to one of the five 1928 reprints. So far as it can in the tiny space allowed, it provided an adequate précis of the plot. After some chat about Shropshire, Baldwin goes on :

> 'She has interlaced with this natural beauty the tragic drama of a youth whose whole being is bent on toil and thrift and worldly success, only to find himself defeated on the morrow of the harvest by the firing of the cornricks by the father of his lover. The dour figure of Gideon Sarn is set against that of his gentle sister, Prudence, who tells the tale. She is a woman flawed with a hare-shotten lip and cursed in the eyes of the neighbours until her soul's loveliness is discerned by Kester Woodseaves, the weaver. And so there comes to her at the end of the story the love which is "the peace to which all hearts do strive".'

Nothing much there to reassure the young intellectuals. Noting, too, that the action takes place at the time of Waterloo, they could have imagined that what the Prime Minister was urging everyone to read was a brew concocted of approximately the same ingredients as those of *The Herries Chronicle*. Many of them did so imagine. And no doubt many of those who bought the book on Baldwin's say-so thought the same, and rejoiced. Both groups grievously underestimated Mary Webb's achievement.

A notable fact of the whole matter is that *Precious Bane* really did contain a lot of elements familiar in the 'Georgian myth'. We have a dour farmer. The father of his loved one is a sinister, half-crazy bogus necromancer. Witchcraft and the powers of darkness, or the belief in them, are as noticeable as Gothic gargoyles. Indeed the heroine is nearly lynched as a spell-binding witch. There are even a bear-baiting and a haughtily immoral rich woman, seeking to seduce the dourly handsome young farmer. Yet it is in part the presence of these elements which illuminates, sometimes luridly, the further fact that this book does not fall into the 'Georgian myth' category at all. To 'escape' into *Precious Bane* would be like escaping into Madame Tussaud's and finding the waxworks, including those in the Chamber of Horrors, alive, sinewy, and most humanly bloody-minded. It would be an experience both stimulating and exhausting. And as you do not know what is to be the outcome of the encounters between these brutally vital figures, the suspense reaches terrible degrees of tension.

Since both the author and the narrator had a harelip – or (in the dialect of the book) a 'hare-shotten' lip – the result of this extreme personal identification might have been expected to be distorting or even mawkish. Not so. Mary Webb's own sufferings are sublimated in those of her heroine so completely that the heroine stands and suffers in, so to speak, her own right : the umbilical cord of the cruel disfigurement has been coolly and expertly cut. The 'happy ending' is a blaze of melo-drama and rich corn. It may be a kind of 'escape', but it comes only just in time to save the strained nerves and over-boiling emotions of the reader.

It has been said, or it certainly ought to have been said, that only a really good model can inspire a really good parody. It is among the achievements of Mary Webb that she, directly in her own books, and indirectly through those of her third-rate imitators, inspired Stella Gibbons's *Cold Comfort Farm*.

Speaking for myself, I still find it mysterious – nearly, indeed, eerie – that Baldwin, even given the sensitive and vigorous guidance of Hamish Hamilton, should have been so right. That, over a period, both he and *Precious Bane* each embodied some 'spirit of the time' may be comfortably stated, and even demonstrated in terms of electoral votes and booksellers' returns. But that there should have been a rapport between the two phenomena? To discover the nature of that inter-relation would demand the sinking of deeper sociological borings than can be undertaken here.

Nor, evidently, did either of them represent the whole spirit, or, one had better say, all the spirits of the time.

For although almost everyone seems able to catalogue this or that literary artefact as 'characteristic of the thirties', the characteristics of that decade were numerous and varied; perhaps even unusually so. In the field of fiction, it would seem that despite the depressed economic conditions of the period, an exceptional number of pretty good novels were circulating pretty well. It may be supposed, given the circumstances of the time, that the proportion of books borrowed to books bought was higher than it had been a few years earlier, and the number of borrowers lining up for each copy allowed by the library's budget was larger. There is no way of proving that.

It might also be supposed that Marxist novelists were having a bonanza in Britain, as a few were beginning to do in the United States. About that something more definite can be said : it was not so. Either the novelists were not there or the readers were not. Expanding that, it could be that the novelists were there all right, but could not find rich publishers. Maybe the readers were there too, but there were not enough publishers with large enough resources to reach them. Gollancz made some forays in that direction, but even the Left Book Club was only marginally concerned with fiction. When it came to choosing serious fiction, the militant worker, the totally and consciously non-Tory British working man, was inclined to look for translations from the Russians, even the nineteenth-century Russians, as being more reliable, and less likely to be hocus-pocused by capitalist ideology.

Among the pretty good novels which sold very well indeed during the thirties one could list, arbitrarily enough, Howard Spring's *Shabby Tiger*, published in 1934, and A. J. Cronin's *The Citadel*, published in 1937. To the obligatory author's

anti-libel note stating that 'all the characters in this book are
purely imaginary', Spring added the words 'There is no such
city as Manchester.' Naturally, the book was all about Manchester and was a vigorous and vehement piece of what I have
heard TV men classify as documentary drama (being related to,
but distinct from, dramatic documentary). It exploited (in the
good sense of the word) that much-exploited city by new and
improved methods. By concentrating on Manchester and thus
sharpening the focus, it achieved, by its particularizations about
Manchester, some valid generalizations about England. The
same could be said, *mutatis mutandis*, about the struggles
against incompetence, dishonesty, and other obstructions and
distractions, of the dedicated doctor in *The Citadel.*

That said, it remains obvious that the generalizations involved
are of a very limited nature. A person could read either of these
books, both examples of what one may cautiously call 'social
naturalism', without more than a faint, and not at all urgent,
awareness of the deep-running, yet increasingly visible, forces
at work in and around the England of the day. One still has the
sense that there is a lot of fog in the Channel and the Continent
has been isolated. There is a notable, even startling difference
here between the literary atmospheres of England and the United
States. The United States is, or certainly was at that time, a
great deal more sensitive to the world's weather than England.
The sense that the System was on the skids, and probably headed
straight for Holocaust II, was far more vivid and obtrusive in
the U.S. than in Britain.

English writers, and other English observers of their home
scene, often explain this by pointing out that the British 'tend
to distrust generalizations', are 'suspicious of Isms', are, if you
want to clinch it, empirical. They will certainly not go overboard for some theory of the nature of society; they shun, it is
said, all forms of philosophizing about Life and History. A Thing
– they claim – is, in the characteristically English view, a
Thing is a Thing.

This is held to explain the peculiarly cautious, circumscribed,
muted reactions of British writers of social-naturalistic fiction to
the gales, blizzards, and thunderclaps of the nineteen-thirties.
This proposition is linked to estimates, probes, and analyses
showing that the British working class is similarly pragmatical,

similarly anti-Ism, as evidenced by its long-term preference for Labourism as against Marxism.

These are useful observations for people to be making. It ought, however, to be borne in mind that, in so far as they are true at all, they are true of only a shortish bit of the road of British history. Applied to any period of modern history earlier than the mid-nineteenth century they make hardly any sense at all.

If the view of British attitudes held by the observers just mentioned is true of the brief period under review, it would suggest that it was in part the rarity of political philosophizing and of Isms in the work of the social-naturalist writers which assisted their appeal to a section of British readers. Their work conveys a subconscious assurance that however ghastly England looks, it is specifically England, and unique, and thus in a not fully defined, but immediately intelligible, way insulated from the world storm. Thus, just possibly, It may never happen here. Such an assurance could provide a relief, if not quite an escape.

As I have suggested, there probably were a lot of people who, on getting the O.K. from Stanley Baldwin, ran for *Precious Bane* feeling confident that at least that book, being set away back in the days of Waterloo, would take them rather further from the disturbing contemporary scene (the book was reprinted twice in the year the British Fleet mutinied) than the social-naturalists were likely to do. The contrary was the case. *Precious Bane*, though set in a particular historical period, was very far from being a 'period piece'. Precisely by shifting her scene back into history, the author, freed from the limitations of the contemporary documentary, left herself scope for a more general, more savage realism.

A high surrealism was the essence of another outstanding spirit of the time; in this case the sort of surrealism sometimes achieved by the circus or a fairground with Giant Dipper, chips, and Dodgems. Creator of this entertainment: Enid Bagnold. Name of book: *National Velvet*. First published 1935, reprinted again and again, most recently in 1970. Summary of plot: fourteen-year-old lower-middle-class girl dreams of entering piebald gelding won in shilling raffle for Grand National and riding it herself. Does so. Wins. Becomes national heroine. End story.

Not any great number of book buyers are fourteen-year-old girls huddled with Pa, ex flyweight boxer, Ma, ex-champion

Channel swimmer, three sisters 'all exactly alike, like golden greyhounds', and a small brother reminiscent of a poltergeist, in a village round which 'unearthly humps of land curved into the darkening sky like the backs of browsing pigs, like the rumps of elephants.' Nor does the book-buyer's family dialogue normally read like a trailer written, all those years beforehand, for a stage scene written by Pinter and Milligan in tight collaboration.

No matter. Scores of thousands of people immediately identified with Velvet Brown, also with her piebald, National Velvet. As a result, they were taken on a brilliantly organized trip through an England in which everything was real enough except the entire situation. It was, some people proudly said at the time, 'the kind of book no foreigner could understand.' In fact it was the kind of book which could best help to make England readily comprehensible to any imaginative outsider.

The book, and its huge popularity, displayed in those decades of stress and menace showed a facet of English mentality, English requirements not much displayed in any of the other bestsellers paraded and examined here. Yet the galloping National Velvet can certainly not be denied its rating as an authentic Spirit of the Time.